GITANJALI AND
FRUIT-GATHERING

THE MACMILLAN COMPANY
NEW YORK · BOSTON · CHICAGO · DALLAS
ATLANTA · SAN FRANCISCO

MACMILLAN & CO., LIMITED
LONDON · BOMBAY · CALCUTTA
MELBOURNE

THE MACMILLAN CO. OF CANADA, LTD.
TORONTO

Painted by Nandalal Bose

GITANJALI AND FRUIT~GATHERING
BY SIR RABINDRANATH TAGORE
WITH ILLUSTRATIONS BY NANDALAL BOSE, SURENDRANATH KAR, ABANINDRANATH TAGORE, AND NOBENDRANATH TAGORE

18-18491

THE MACMILLAN COMPANY
NEW~YORK

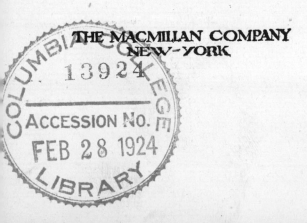

Norwood Press
J. S. Cushing Co. — Berwick & Smith Co.
Norwood, Mass., U.S.A.

TO

WILLIAM ROTHENSTEIN

INTRODUCTION

A FEW days ago I said to a distin-
guished Bengali doctor of medicine, "I
know no German, yet if a translation of
a German poet had moved me, I would
go to the British Museum and find
books in English that would tell me
something of his life, and of the history
of his thought. But though these prose
translations from Rabindranath Tagore
have stirred my blood as nothing has
for years, I shall not know anything
of his life, and of the movements of
thought that have made them possible,
if some Indian traveller will not tell
me." It seemed to him natural that I
should be moved, for he said, "I read

Rabindranath every day, to read one
line of his is to forget all the troubles
of the world. " I said,"An Englishman
living in London in the reign of Richard
the Second had he been shown translations from Petrarch or from Dante,
would have found no books to answer
his questions, but would have questioned some Florentine banker or Lom-
bard merchant as I question you. For
all I know, so abundant and simple is
this poetry, the new Renaissance has
been born in your country and I shall
never know of it except by hearsay."
He answered, "We have other poets,
but none that are his equal; we call this
the epoch of Rabindranath. No poet
seems to me as famous in Europe as
he is among us. He is as great in
music as in poetry, and his songs are
sung from the west of India into Bur-
mah wherever Bengali is spoken. He
was already famous at nineteen when

he wrote his first novel; and plays,
written when he was but little older,
are still played in Calcutta. I so much
admire the completeness of his life;
when he was very young he wrote
much of natural objects, he would sit
all day in his garden; from his twenty-
fifth year or so to his thirty-fifth perhaps, when he had a great sorrow, he
wrote the most beautiful love poetry
in our language"; and then he said with
deep emotion, "words can never ex-
press what I owed at seventeen to his
love poetry. After that his art grew
deeper, it became religious and philo-
sophical; all the aspirations of man-
kind are in his hymns. He is the first
among our saints who has not refused
to live, but has spoken out of Life itself, and that is why we give him our
love." I may have changed his well
chosen words in my memory but not
his thought. "A little while ago he

was to read divine service in one of
our churches—we of the Brahma Samaj
use your word 'church' in English—it
,was the largest in Calcutta and not
only was it crowded, people even standing in the windows, but the streets
were all but impassable because of the
people."

Other Indians came to see me and
their reverence for this man sounded
strange in our world, where we hide
great and little things under the same
veil of obvious comedy and half-serious
depreciation. When we were making
the cathedrals had we a like reverence
for our great men? "Every morning
at three—I know, for I have seen it"—
one said to me, "he sits immovable in
contemplation, and for two hours does
not awake from his reverie upon the
nature of God. His father, the Maha
Rishi, would sometimes sit there all
through the next day; once, upon a

river, he fell into contemplation because of the beauty of the landscape, and the rowers waited for eight hours before they could continue their journey." He then told me of Mr. Tagore's family and how for generations great men have come out of its cradles. "To-day," he said, "there are Gogonendranath and Abanindranath Tagore, who are artists; and Dwijendranath, Rabindranath's brother, who is a great philosopher. The squirrels come from the boughs and climb on to his knees and the birds alight upon his hands." I notice in these men's thought a sense of visible beauty and meaning as though they held that doctrine of Nietzsche that we must not believe in the moral or intellectual beauty which does not sooner or later impress itself upon physical things. I said, "In the East you know how to keep a family illustrious. The other day the curator of a

Museum pointed out to me a little
dark-skinned man who was arranging
their Chinese prints and said, 'That
is the hereditary connoisseur of the
Mikado, he is the fourteenth of his
family to hold the post.'" He answered. "When Rabindranath was a
boy he had all round him in his home
literature and music." I thought of
the abundance, of the simplicity of the
poems, and said, "In your country
is there much propagandist writing,
much criticism? We have to do so
much, especially in my own country,
that our minds gradually cease to be
creative, and yet we cannot help it. If
our life was not a continual warfare, we
would not have taste, we would not
know what is good, we would not find
hearers and readers. Four-fifths of our
energy is spent in the quarrel with bad
taste, whether in our own minds or in
the minds of others." "I understand,"

he replied, "we too have our propagandist writing. In the villages they recite long mythological poems adapted from the Sanscrit in the Middle Ages, and they often insert passages telling the people that they must do their duties.

II

I have carried the manuscript of these translations about with me for days, reading it in railway trains, or on the tops of omnibuses and in restaurants, and I have often had to close it lest some stranger would see how much it moved me. These lyrics—which are in the original, my Indians tell me, full of subtlety of rhythm, of untranslatable delicacies of colour, of metrical invention—display in their thought a world I have dreamed of all my life long. The work of a supreme culture, they yet appear as

much the growth of the common soil
as the grass and the rushes. A tradi-
tion, where poetry and religion are
the same thing, has passed through the
centuries, gathering from learned and
unlearned metaphor and emotion, and
carried back again to the multitude
the thought of the scholar and of the
noble. If the civilization of Bengal
remains unbroken, if that common
mind which—as one divines—runs
through all, is not, as with us, broken
into a dozen minds that know nothing
of each other, something even of what
is most subtle in these verses will have
come, in a few generations, to the
beggar on the roads. When there
was but one mind in England Chaucer
wrote his *Troilus and Cressida*, and
though he had written to be read, or
to be read out—for our time was
coming on apace—he was sung by
minstrels for a while. Rabindranath

Tagore, like Chaucer's forerunners,
writes music for his words, and one
understands at every moment that he
is so abundant, so spontaneous, so
daring in his passion, so full of surprise,
because he is doing something which
has never seemed strange, unnatural,
or in need of defence. These verses
will not lie in little well-printed books
upon ladies' tables, who turn the pages
with indolent hands that they may
sigh over a life without meaning,
which is yet all they can know of life,
or be carried about by students at the
university to be laid aside when the
work of life begins, but as the generations pass, travellers will hum them
on the highway and men rowing upon
rivers. Lovers, while they await one
another, shall find, in murmuring them,
this love of God a magic gulf wherein
their own more bitter passion may
bathe and renew its youth. At every

moment the heart of this poet flows
outward to these without derogation or
condescension, for it has known that
they will understand; and it has filled
itself with the circumstance of their
lives. The traveller in the red-brown
clothes that he wears that dust may
not show upon him, the girl searching
in her bed for the petals fallen from
the wreath of her royal lover, the
servant or the bride awaiting the
master's home-coming in the empty
house, are images of the heart turning
to God. Flowers and rivers, the
blowing of conch shells, the heavy rain
of the Indian July, or the parching
heat, are images of the moods of that
heart in union or in separation; and
a man sitting in a boat upon a river
playing upon a lute, like one of those
figures full of mysterious meaning in
a Chinese picture, is God Himself.
A whole people, a whole civilization,

immeasurably strange to us, seems to
have been taken up into this imagina-
tion; and yet we are not moved because of its strangeness, but because
we have met our own image, as though
we had walked in Rossetti's willow
wood, or heard, perhaps for the first
time in literature, our voice as in a
dream.

Since the Renaissance the writing of
European saints—however familiar
their metaphor and the general struc-
ture of their thought—has ceased to
hold our attention. We know that we
must at last forsake the world, and we
are accustomed in moments of weariness or exaltation to consider a volun-
tary forsaking; but how can we, who
have read so much poetry, seen so many
paintings, listened to so much music,
where the cry of the flesh and the cry
of the soul seem one, forsake it harshly
and rudely? What have we in common

with St. Bernard covering his eyes that
they may not dwell upon the beauty of
the lakes of Switzerland, or with the
violent rhetoric of the Book of Revela-
tion? We would, if we might, find,
as in this book, words full of courtesy.
"I have got my leave. Bid me farewell, my brothers! I bow to you all
and take my departure. Here I give
back the keys of my door—and I give
up all claims to my house. I only ask
for last kind words from you. We
were neighbours for long, but I received
more than I could give. Now the day
has dawned and the lamp that lit my
dark corner is out. A summons has
come and I am ready for my journey."
And it is our own mood, when it is
furthest from À Kempis or John of the
Cross, that cries, "And because I love
this life, I know I shall love death
as well." Yet it is not only in our
thoughts of the parting that this book

INTRODUCTION

fathoms all. We had not known that
we loved God, hardly it may be that
we believed in Him; yet looking back-
ward upon our life we discover, in our
exploration of the pathways of woods,
in our delight in the lonely places of
hills, in that mysterious claim that we
have made, unavailingly, on the women
that we have loved, the emotion that
created this insidious sweetness. "Entering my heart unbidden even as
one of the common crowd, unknown
to me, my king, thou didst press the
signet of eternity upon many a fleeting moment," This is no longer the
sanctity of the cell and of the scourge;
being but a lifting up, as it were, into a
greater intensity of the mood of the
painter, painting the dust and the sun-
light, and we go for a like voice to St.
Francis and to William Blake who
have seemed so alien in our violent
history.

III

We write long books where no page perhaps has any quality to make writing a pleasure, being confident in some general design, just as we fight and make money and fill our heads with politics—all dull things in the doing—while Mr. Tagore, like the Indian civilization itself, has been content to discover the soul and surrender himself to its spontaneity. He often seems to contrast his life with that of those who have lived more after our fashion, and have more seeming weight in the world, and always humbly as though he were only sure his way is best for him: "Men going home glance at me and smile and fill me with shame. I sit like a beggar maid, drawing my skirt over my face, and when they ask me, what it is I want, I drop

my eyes and answer them not." At
another time, remembering how his life
had once a different shape, he will say,
"Many an hour have I spent in the
strife of the good and the evil, but now
it is the pleasure of my playmate of
the empty days to draw my heart on
to him; and I know not why is this
sudden call to what useless inconsc-
quence." An innocence, a simplicity
that one does not find elsewhere in
literature makes the birds and the
leaves seem as near to him as they are
near to children, and the changes of
the seasons great events as before our
thoughts had arisen between them and
us. At times I wonder if he has it
from the literature of Bengal or from
religion, and at other times, remembering the birds alighting on his brother's
hands, I find pleasure in thinking it
hereditary, a mystery that was growing
through the centuries like the courtesy

of a Tristan or a Pelanore. Indeed,
when he is speaking of children, so
much a part of himself this quality
seems, one is not certain that he is not
also speaking of the saints, "They build
their houses with sand and they play
with empty shells. With withered
leaves they weave their boats and
smilingly float them on the vast deep.
Children have their play on the seashore of worlds. They know not how
to swim, they know not how to cast
nets. Pearl fishers dive for pearls,
merchants sail in their ships, while
children gather pebbles and scatter
them again. They seek not for hidden
treasures, they know not how to cast
nets."

W. B. YEATS.

September 1912.

CONTENTS

ILLUSTRATIONS IN COLOUR

ILLUSTRATIONS IN BLACK AND WHITE

GITANJALI

I

Thou hast made me endless, such is thy pleasure. This frail vessel thou emptiest again and again, and fillest it ever with fresh life.

This little flute of a reed thou hast carried over hills and dales, and hast breathed through it melodies eternally new.

At the immortal touch of thy hands my little heart loses its limits in joy and gives birth to utterance ineffable.

Thy infinite gifts come to me only on these very small hands of mine. Ages pass, and still thou pourest, and still there is room to fill.

2

WHEN thou commandest me to sing it seems that my heart would break with pride; and I look to thy face, and tears come to my eyes.

All that is harsh and dissonant in my life melts into one sweet harmony —and my adoration spreads wings like a glad bird on its flight across the sea.

I know thou takest pleasure in my singing. I know that only as a singer I come before thy presence.

I touch by the edge of the far spreading wing of my song thy feet which I could never aspire to reach.

Drunk with the joy of singing I forget myself and call thee friend who art my lord.

3

I KNOW not how thou singest, my master! I ever listen in silent amazement.

The light of thy music illumines the world. The life breath of thy music runs from sky to sky. The holy stream of thy music breaks through all stony obstacles and rushes on.

My heart longs to join in thy song, but vainly struggles for a voice. I would speak, but speech breaks not into song, and I cry out baffled. Ah, thou hast made my heart captive in the endless meshes of thy music, my master!

4

LIFE of my life, I shall ever try to keep my body pure, knowing that thy living touch is upon all my limbs.

I shall ever try to keep all untruths

out from my thoughts, knowing that
thou art that truth which has kindled
the light of reason in my mind.

I shall ever try to drive all evils away
from my heart and keep my love in
flower, knowing that thou hast thy seat
in the inmost shrine of my heart.

And it shall be my endeavour to
reveal thee in my actions, knowing it
is thy power gives me strength to act.

5

I ASK for a moment's indulgence to sit
by thy side. The works that I have
in hand I will finish afterwards.

Away from the sight of thy face my
heart knows no rest nor respite, and
my work becomes an endless toil in a
shoreless sea of toil.

To-day the summer has come at my
window with its sighs and murmurs;

and the bees are plying their minstrelsy
at the court of the flowering grove.

Now it is time to sit quiet, face to
face with thee, and to sing dedication
of life in this silent and overflowing
leisure.

6

PLUCK this little flower and take it,
delay not! I fear lest it droop and
drop into the dust.

It may not find a place in thy garland, but honour it with a touch of
pain from thy hand and pluck it. I
fear lest the day end before I am
aware, and the time of offering go by.

Though its colour be not deep and
its smell be faint, use this flower in
thy service and pluck it while there
is time.

7

My song has put off her adornments.
She has no pride of dress and decora-
tion. Ornaments would mar our union;
they would come between thee and
me; their jingling would drown thy
whispers.

My poet's vanity dies in shame before
thy sight. O master poet, I have sat
down at thy feet. Only let me make
my life simple and straight, like a flute
of reed for thee to fill with music.

8

The child who is decked with prince's
robes and who has jewelled chains
round his neck loses all pleasure in his
play; his dress hampers him at every
step.

In fear that it may be frayed, or

Drawn by Nandalal Bose

My song has put off her adornments

stained with dust he keeps himself from the world, and is afraid even to move.

Mother, it is no gain, thy bondage of finery, if it keep one shut off from the healthful dust of the earth, if it rob one of the right of entrance to the great fair of common human life.

9

O FOOL, to try to carry thyself upon thy own shoulders! O beggar, to come to beg at thy own door!

Leave all thy burdens on his hands who can bear all, and never look behind in regret.

Thy desire at once puts out the light from the lamp it touches with its breath. It is unholy—take not thy gifts through its unclean hands. Accept only what is offered by sacred love.

10

HERE is thy footstool and there rest thy feet where live the poorest, and lowliest, and lost.

When I try to bow to thee, my obeisance cannot reach down to the depth where thy feet rest among the poorest, and lowliest, and lost.

Pride can never approach to where thou walkest in the clothes of the humble among the poorest, and lowliest, and lost.

My heart can never find its way to where thou keepest company with the companionless among the poorest, the lowliest, and the lost.

11

LEAVE this chanting and singing and telling of beads! Whom dost thou worship in this lonely dark corner of a

Painted by Nandalal Bose

Leave this chanting and singing

temple with doors all shut? Open thine eyes and see thy God is not before thee!

He is there where the tiller is tilling the hard ground and where the path-maker is breaking stones. He is with them in sun and in shower, and his garment is covered with dust. Put off thy holy mantle and even like him come down on the dusty soil!

Deliverance? Where is this deliverance to be found? Our master himself has joyfully taken upon him the bonds of creation; he is bound with us all for ever.

Come out of thy meditations and leave aside thy flowers and incense! What harm is there if thy clothes become tattered and stained? Meet him and stand by him in toil and in sweat of thy brow.

12

THE time that my journey takes is long and the way of it long.

I came out on the chariot of the first gleam of light, and pursued my voyage through the wildernesses of worlds leaving my track on many a star and planet.

It is the most distant course that comes nearest to thyself, and that training is the most intricate which leads to the utter simplicity of a tune.

The traveller has to knock at every alien door to come to his own, and one has to wander through all the outer worlds to reach the innermost shrine at the end.

My eyes strayed far and wide before I shut them and said "Here art thou!"

The question and the cry "Oh, where?" melt into tears of a thousand streams and deluge the world with the flood of the assurance "I am!"

Painted by Surendranath Kar

Here is thy footstool

13

THE song that I came to sing remains unsung to this day.

I have spent my days in stringing and in unstringing my instrument.

The time has not come true, the words have not been rightly set; only there is the agony of wishing in my heart.

The blossom has not opened; only the wind is sighing by.

I have not seen his face, nor have I listened to his voice; only I have heard his gentle footsteps from the road before my house.

The livelong day has passed in spreading his seat on the floor; but the lamp has not been lit and I cannot ask him into my house.

I live in the hope of meeting with him; but this meeting is not yet.

14

My desires are many and my cry is pitiful, but ever didst thou save me by hard refusals; and this strong mercy has been wrought into my life through and through.

Day by day thou art making me worthy of the simple, great gifts that thou gavest to me unasked—this sky and the light, this body and the life and the mind—saving me from perils of overmuch desire.

There are times when I languidly linger and times when I awaken and hurry in search of my goal; but cruelly thou hidest thyself from before me.

Day by day thou art making me worthy of thy full acceptance by refusing me ever and anon, saving me from perils of weak, uncertain desire.

Drawn by Nandalal Bose

The Song that I came to sing

15

I AM here to sing thee songs. In this hall of thine I have a corner seat.

In thy world I have no work to do; my useless life can only break out in tunes without a purpose.

When the hour strikes for thy silent worship at dark temple of midnight, command me, my master, to stand before thee to sing.

When in the morning air the golden harp is tuned, honour me, commanding my presence.

16

I HAVE had my invitation to this world's festival, and thus my life has been blessed. My eyes have seen and my ears have heard.

It was my part at this feast to play upon my instrument, and I have done all I could.

Now, I ask, has the time come at last when I may go in and see thy face and offer thee my silent salutation?

17

I AM only waiting for love to give myself up at last into his hands. That is why it is so late and why I have been guilty of such omissions.

They come with their laws and their codes to bind me fast; but I evade them ever, for I am only waiting for love to give myself up at last into his hands.

People blame me and call me heed-less; I doubt not they are right in their blame.

The market day is over and work is all done for the busy. Those who came to call me in vain have gone back in anger. I am only waiting for love to give myself up at last into his hands.

18

CLOUDS heap upon clouds and it darkens. Ah, love, why dost thou let me wait outside at the door all alone?

In the busy moments of the noontide work I am with the crowd, but on this dark lonely day it is only for thee that I hope.

If thou showest me not thy face, if thou leavest me wholly aside, I know not how I am to pass these long, rainy hours.

I keep gazing on the far away gloom of the sky, and my heart wanders wailing with the restless wind.

19

IF thou speakest not I will fill my heart with thy silence and endure it. I will keep still and wait like the night with starry vigil and its head bent low with patience.

The morning will surely come, the darkness will vanish, and thy voice pour down in golden streams breaking through the sky.

Then thy words will take wing in songs from every one of my birds' nests, and thy melodies will break forth in flowers in all my forest groves.

20

On the day when the lotus bloomed, alas, my mind was straying, and I knew it not. My basket was empty and the flower remained unheeded.

Only now and again a sadness fell upon me, and I started up from my dream and felt a sweet trace of a strange fragrance in the south wind.

That vague sweetness made my heart ache with longing and it seemed to me that it was the eager breath of the summer seeking for its completion.

I knew not then that it was so near, that it was mine, and that this perfect sweetness had blossomed in the depth of my own heart.

21

I MUST launch out my boat. The languid hours pass by on the shore— Alas for me!

The spring has done its flowering and taken leave. And now with the burden of faded futile flowers I wait and linger.

The waves have become clamorous, and upon the bank in the shady lane the yellow leaves flutter and fall.

What emptiness do you gaze upon! Do you not feel a thrill passing through the air with the notes of the far away song floating from the other shore?

22

IN the deep shadows of the rainy July, with secret steps, thou walkest, silent as night, eluding all watchers.

To-day the morning has closed its eyes, heedless of the insistent calls of the loud east wind, and a thick veil has been drawn over the ever-wakeful blue sky.

The woodlands have hushed their songs, and doors are all shut at every house. Thou art the solitary wayfarer in this deserted street. Oh my only friend, my best beloved, the gates are open in my house—do not pass by like a dream.

23

ART thou abroad on this stormy night on the journey of love, my friend? The sky groans like one in despair.

I have no sleep to-night. Ever and

Painted by Nandalal Bose

Art thou abroad on this stormy night?

again I open my door and look out on
the darkness, my friend!

I can see nothing before me. I
wonder where lies thy path!

By what dim shore of the ink-black
river, by what far edge of the frowning
forest, through what mazy depth of
gloom art thou threading thy course
to come to me, my friend?

24

IF the day is done, if birds sing no
more, if the wind has flagged tired,
then draw the veil of darkness thick
upon me, even as thou hast wrapt the
earth with the coverlet of sleep and
tenderly closed the petals of the drooping lotus at dusk.

From the traveller, whose sack of
provisions is empty before the voyage
is ended, whose garment is torn and
dust-laden, whose strength is ex-

hausted, remove shame and poverty,
and renew his life like a flower under
the cover of thy kindly night.

25

In the night of weariness let me give
myself up to sleep without struggle,
resting my trust upon thee.

Let me not force my flagging spirit
into a poor preparation for thy worship.

It is thou who drawest the veil of
night upon the tired eyes of the day to
renew its sight in a fresher gladness of
awakening.

26

He came and sat by my side but I
woke not. What a cursed sleep it was,
O miserable me!

He came when the night was still;
he had his harp in his hands, and
my dreams became resonant with its
melodies.

Alas, why are my nights all thus lost? Ah, why do I ever miss his sight whose breath touches my sleep?

27

LIGHT, oh where is the light? Kindle it with the burning fire of desire!

There is the lamp but never a flicker of a flame,—is such thy fate, my heart! Ah, death were better by far for thee!

Misery knocks at thy door, and her message is that thy lord is wakeful, and he calls thee to thy love-tryst through the darkness of night.

The sky is overcast with clouds and the rain is ceaseless. I know not what this is that stirs in me,—I know not its meaning.

A moment's flash of lightning drags down a deeper gloom on my sight, and my heart gropes for the path to where the music of the night calls me.

Light, oh where is the light! Kindle it with the burning fire of desire! It thunders and the wind rushes screaming through the void. The night is black as a black stone. Let not the hours pass by in the dark. Kindle the lamp of love with thy life.

28

OBSTINATE are the trammels, but my heart aches when I try to break them.

Freedom is all I want, but to hope for it I feel ashamed.

I am certain that priceless wealth is in thee, and that thou art my best friend, but I have not the heart to sweep away the tinsel that fills my room.

The shroud that covers me is a shroud of dust and death; I hate it, yet hug it in love.

My debts are large, my failures great,

my shame secret and heavy; yet when I come to ask for my good, I quake in fear lest my prayer be granted.

29

HE whom I enclose with my name is weeping in this dungeon. I am ever busy building this wall all around; and as this wall goes up into the sky day by day I lose sight of my true being in its dark shadow.

I take pride in this great wall, and I plaster it with dust and sand lest a least hole should be left in this name; and for all the care I take I lose sight of my true being.

30

I CAME out alone on my way to my tryst. But who is this that follows me in the silent dark?

I move aside to avoid his presence but I escape him not.

He makes the dust rise from the earth with his swagger; he adds his loud voice to every word that I utter.

He is my own little self, my lord, he knows no shame; but I am ashamed to come to thy door in his company.

31

"Prisoner, tell me, who was it that bound you?"

"It was my master," said the prisoner. "I thought I could outdo everybody in the world in wealth and power, and I amassed in my own treasure-house the money due to my king. When sleep overcame me I lay upon the bed that was for my lord, and on waking up I found I was a prisoner in my own treasure-house."

Painted by Abanindranath Tagore

Prisoners, tell me, who was it that bound you?

"Prisoner, tell me who was it that wrought this unbreakable chain?"

"It was I," said the prisoner, "who forged this chain very carefully. I thought my invincible power would hold the world captive leaving me in a freedom undisturbed. Thus night and day I worked at the chain with huge fires and cruel hard strokes. When at last the work was done and the links were complete and unbreakable, I found that it held me in its grip."

32

By all means they try to hold me secure who love me in this world. But it is otherwise with thy love which is greater than theirs, and thou keepest me free.

Lest I forget them they never venture to leave me alone. But day passes by after day and thou art not seen.

If I call not thee in my prayers, if I keep not thee in my heart, thy love for me still waits for my love.

33

WHEN it was day they came into my house and said, "We shall only take the smallest room here."

They said, "We shall help you in the worship of your God and humbly accept only our own share of his grace"; and then they took their seat in a corner and they sat quiet and meek.

But in the darkness of night I find they break into my sacred shrine, strong and turbulent, and snatch with unholy greed the offerings from God's altar.

34

LET only that little be left of me whereby I may name thee my all.

Let only that little be left of my will whereby I may feel thee on every side, and come to thee in everything, and offer to thee my love every moment.

Let only that little be left of me whereby I may never hide thee.

Let only that little of my fetters be left whereby I am bound with thy will, and thy purpose is carried out in my life—and that is the fetter of thy love.

35

WHERE the mind is without fear and the head is held high;

Where knowledge is free;

Where the world has not been broken up into fragments by narrow domestic walls;

Where words come out from the depth of truth;

Where tireless striving stretches its arms towards perfection;

Where the clear stream of reason has
not lost its way into the dreary desert
sand of dead habit;

Where the mind is led forward by
thee into ever-widening thought and
action—

Into that heaven of freedom, my
Father, let my country awake.

36

THIS is my prayer to thee, my lord—
strike, strike at the root of penury in
my heart.

Give me the strength lightly to bear
my joys and sorrows.

Give me the strength to make my
love fruitful in service.

Give me the strength never to disown
the poor or bend my knees before
insolent might.

Give me the strength to raise my
mind high above daily trifles.

And give me the strength to surrender my strength to thy will with love.

37

I THOUGHT that my voyage had come to its end at the last limit of my power, —that the path before me was closed, that provisions were exhausted and the time come to take shelter in a silent obscurity.

But I find that thy will knows no end in me. And when old words die out on the tongue, new melodies break forth from the heart; and where the old tracks are lost, new country is revealed with its wonders.

38

THAT I want thee, only thee—let my heart repeat without end. All desires that distract me, day and night, are false and empty to the core.

As the night keeps hidden in its gloom the petition for light, even thus in the depth of my unconsciousness rings the cry—I want thee, only thee.

As the storm still seeks its end in peace when it strikes against peace with all its might, even thus my rebellion strikes against thy love and still its cry is—I want thee, only thee.

39

WHEN the heart is hard and parched up, come upon me with a shower of mercy.

When grace is lost from life, come with a burst of song.

When tumultuous work raises its din on all sides shutting me out from beyond, come to me, my lord of silence, with thy peace and rest.

When my beggarly heart sits crouched, shut up in a corner, break

Painted by Abanindranath Tagore

The rain has held back for days

open the door, my king, and come with
the ceremony of a king.

When desire blinds the mind with
delusion and dust, O thou holy one,
thou wakeful, come with thy light and
thy thunder.

40

THE rain has held back for days and
days, my God, in my arid heart. The
horizon is fiercely naked—not the thin-
nest cover of a soft cloud, not the
vaguest hint of a distant cool shower.

Send thy angry storm, dark with
death, if it is thy wish, and with lashes
of lightning startle the sky from end to
end.

But call back, my lord, call back
this pervading silent heat, still and keen
and cruel, burning the heart with dire
despair.

Let the cloud of grace bend low from

above like the tearful look of the mother
on the day of the father's wrath.

41

WHERE dost thou stand behind them
all, my lover, hiding thyself in the
shadows? They push thee and pass
thee by on the dusty road, taking thee
for naught. I wait here weary hours
spreading my offerings for thee, while
passers by come and take my flowers,
one by one, and my basket is nearly
empty.

The morning time is past, and the
noon. In the shade of evening my
eyes are drowsy with sleep. Men going
home glance at me and smile and fill
me with shame. I sit like a beggar
maid, drawing my skirt over my face,
and when they ask me, what it is I
want, I drop my eyes and answer them
not.

Oh, how, indeed, could I tell them that for thee I wait, and that thou hast promised to come. How could I utter for shame that I keep for my dowry this poverty. Ah, I hug this pride in the secret of my heart.

I sit on the grass and gaze upon the sky and dream of the sudden splendour of thy coming—all the lights ablaze, golden pennons flying over thy car, and they at the roadside standing agape, when they see thee come down from thy seat to raise me from the dust, and set at thy side this ragged beggar girl a-tremble with shame and pride, like a creeper in a summer breeze.

But time glides on and still no sound of the wheels of thy chariot. Many a procession passes by with noise and shouts and glamour of glory. Is it only thou who wouldst stand in the shadow silent and behind them all? And only I

who would wait and weep and wear out
my heart in vain longing?

42

EARLY in the day it was whispered that
we should sail in a boat, only thou and
I, and never a soul in the world would
know of this our pilgrimage to no
country and to no end.

In that shoreless ocean, at thy silently
listening smile my songs would swell
in melodies, free as waves, free from all
bondage of words.

Is the time not come yet? Are there
works still to do? Lo, the evening
has come down upon the shore and in
the fading light the seabirds come
flying to their nests.

Who knows when the chains will be
off, and the boat, like the last glimmer
of sunset, vanish into the night?

43

THE day was when I did not keep myself in readiness for thee; and entering my heart unbidden even as one of the common crowd, unknown to me, my king, thou didst press the signet of eternity upon many a fleeting moment of my life.

And to-day when by chance I light upon them and see thy signature, I find they have lain scattered in the dust mixed with the memory of joys and sorrows of my trivial days forgotten.

Thou didst not turn in contempt from my childish play among dust, and the steps that I heard in my playroom are the same that are echoing from star to star.

44

THIS is my delight, thus to wait and watch at the wayside where shadow chases light and the rain comes in the wake of the summer.

Messengers, with tidings from unknown skies, greet me and speed along the road. My heart is glad within, and the breath of the passing breeze is sweet.

From dawn till dusk I sit here before my door, and I know that of a sudden the happy moment will arrive when I shall see.

In the meanwhile I smile and I sing all alone. In the meanwhile the air is filling with the perfume of promise.

45

HAVE you not heard his silent steps? He comes, comes, ever comes.

Painted by Abanindranath Tagore

Have you not heard his silent steps?

Every moment and every age, every
day and every night he comes, comes,
ever comes.

Many a song have I sung in many a
mood of mind, but all their notes have
always proclaimed, "He comes, comes,
ever comes."

In the fragrant days of sunny April
through the forest path he comes,
comes, ever comes.

In the rainy gloom of July nights on
the thundering chariot of clouds he
comes, comes, ever comes.

In sorrow after sorrow it is his steps
that press upon my heart, and it is
the golden touch of his feet that
makes my joy to shine.

46

I KNOW not from what distant time
thou art ever coming nearer to meet

me. Thy sun and stars can never
keep thee hidden from me for aye.

In many a morning and eve thy
footsteps have been heard and thy
messenger has come within my heart
and called me in secret.

I know not why to-day my life is all
astir, and a feeling of tremulous joy is
passing through my heart.

It is as if the time were come to
wind up my work, and I feel in the air
a faint smell of thy sweet presence.

47

THE night is nearly spent waiting for
him in vain. I fear lest in the morning
he suddenly come to my door when I
have fallen asleep wearied out. Oh
friends, leave the way open to him—
forbid him not.

If the sound of his steps does not
wake me, do not try to rouse me, I

pray. I wish not to be called from my
sleep by the clamorous choir of birds,
by the riot of wind at the festival of
morning light. Let me sleep undisturbed even if my lord comes of a
sudden to my door.

Ah, my sleep, precious sleep, which
only waits for his touch to vanish.
Ah, my closed eyes that would open
their lids to the light of his smile
when he stands before me like a dream
emerging from darkness of sleep.

Let him appear before my sight as
the first of all lights and all forms.
The first thrill of joy to my awakened
soul let it come from his glance. And
let my return to myself be immediate
return to him.

48

THE morning sea of silence broke into
ripples of bird songs; and the flowers

were all merry by the roadside; and
the wealth of gold was scattered
through the rift of the clouds while
we busily went on our way and paid no
heed.

We sang no glad songs nor played;
we went not to the village for barter;
we spoke not a word nor smiled;
we lingered not on the way. We
quickened our pace more and more as
the time sped by.

The sun rose to the mid sky and
doves cooed in the shade. Withered
leaves danced and whirled in the hot
air of noon. The shepherd boy drowsed
and dreamed in the shadow of the
banyan tree, and I laid myself down
by the water and stretched my tired
limbs on the grass.

My companions laughed at me in
scorn; they held their heads high and
hurried on; they never looked back nor
rested; they vanished in the distant blue

haze. They crossed many meadows and hills, and passed through strange, far-away countries. All honour to you, heroic host of the interminable path! Mockery and reproach pricked me to rise, but found no response in me. I gave myself up for lost in the depth of a glad humiliation—in the shadow of a dim delight.

The repose of the sun-embroidered green gloom slowly spread over my heart. I forgot for what I had travelled, and I surrendered my mind without struggle to the maze of shadows and songs.

At last, when I woke from my slumber and opened my eyes, I saw thee standing by me, flooding my sleep with thy smile. How I had feared that the path was long and wearisome, and the struggle to reach thee was hard!

49

You came down from your throne and stood at my cottage door.

I was singing all alone in a corner, and the melody caught your ear. You came down and stood at my cottage door.

Masters are many in your hall, and songs are sung there at all hours. But the simple carol of this novice struck at your love. One plaintive little strain mingled with the great music of the world, and with a flower for a prize you came down and stopped at my cottage door.

50

I HAD gone a-begging from door to door in the village path, when thy golden chariot appeared in the distance like a gorgeous dream and I wondered who was this King of all kings!

My hopes rose high and methought my evil days were at an end, and I stood waiting for alms to be given unasked and for wealth scattered on all sides in the dust.

The chariot stopped where I stood. Thy glance fell on me and thou camest down with a smile. I felt that the luck of my life had come at last. Then of a sudden thou didst hold out thy right hand and say "What hast thou to give to me?"

Ah, what a kingly jest was it to open thy palm to a beggar to beg! I was confused and stood undecided, and then from my wallet I slowly took out the least little grain of corn and gave it to thee.

But how great my surprise when at the day's end I emptied my bag on the floor to find a least little grain of gold among the poor heap. I bitterly wept and wished that I had had the heart to give thee my all.

51

THE night darkened. Our day's works had been done. We thought that the last guest had arrived for the night and the doors in the village were all shut. Only some said, The king was to come. We laughed and said "No, it cannot be!"

It seemed there were knocks at the door and we said it was nothing but the wind. We put out the lamps and lay down to sleep. Only some said, "It is the messenger!" We laughed and said "No, it must be the wind!"

There came a sound in the dead of the night. We sleepily thought it was the distant thunder. The earth shook, the walls rocked, and it troubled us in our sleep. Only some said, it was the sound of wheels. We said in a drowsy murmur, "No, it must be the rumbling of clouds!"

The night was still dark when the drum sounded. The voice came "Wake up! delay not!" We pressed our hands on our hearts and shuddered with fear. Some said, "Lo, there is the king's flag!" We stood up on our feet and cried "There is no time for delay!"

The king has come—but where are lights, where are wreaths? Where is the throne to seat him? Oh, shame! Oh utter shame! Where is the hall, the decorations? Some one has said, "Vain is this cry! Greet him with empty hands, lead him into thy rooms all bare!"

Open the doors, let the conch-shells be sounded! In the depth of the night has come the king of our dark, dreary house. The thunder roars in the sky. The darkness shudders with lightning. Bring out thy tattered piece of mat and spread it in the courtyard. With the storm has come

of a sudden our king of the fearful
night.

52

I THOUGHT I should ask of thee—but
I dared not—the rose wreath thou
hadst on thy neck. Thus I waited
for the morning, when thou didst
depart, to find a few fragments on the
bed. And like a beggar I searched
in the dawn only for a stray petal or
two.

Ah me, what is it I find? What
token left of thy love? It is no
flower, no spices, no vase of perfumed
water. It is thy mighty sword,
flashing as a flame, heavy as a bolt
of thunder. The young light of
morning comes through the window
and spreads itself upon thy bed. The
morning bird twitters and asks,
"Woman, what hast thou got?" No,

it is no flower, nor spices, nor vase of
perfumed water—it is thy dreadful
sword.

I sit and muse in wonder, what gift
is this of thine. I can find no place
where to hide it. I am ashamed to
wear it, frail as I am, and it hurts me
when I press it to my bosom. Yet
shall I bear in my heart this honour
of the burden of pain, this gift of thine.

From now there shall be no fear
left for me in this world, and thou
shalt be victorious in all my strife.
Thou hast left death for my companion
and I shall crown him with my life.
Thy sword is with me to cut asunder
my bonds, and there shall be no fear
left for me in the world.

From now I leave off all petty
decorations. Lord of my heart, no
more shall there be for me waiting and
weeping in corners, no more coyness
and sweetness of demeanour. Thou

hast given me thy sword for adornment.
No more doll's decorations for me!

53

BEAUTIFUL is thy wristlet, decked
with stars and cunningly wrought in
myriad-coloured jewels. But more
beautiful to me thy sword with its
curve of lightning like the outspread
wings of the divine bird of Vishnu,
perfectly poised in the angry red light
of the sunset.

It quivers like the one last response
of life in ecstasy of pain at the final
stroke of death; it shines like the pure
flame of being burning up earthly sense
with one fierce flash.

Beautiful is thy wristlet, decked
with starry gems; but thy sword, O
lord of thunder, is wrought with
uttermost beauty, terrible to behold
or to think of.

Painted by Nandalal Bose

I asked nothing from thee

54

I ASKED nothing from thee; I uttered not my name to thine ear. When thou took'st thy leave I stood silent. I was alone by the well where the shadow of the tree fell aslant, and the women had gone home with their brown earthen pitchers full to the brim. They called me and shouted, "Come with us, the morning is wearing on to noon." But I languidly lingered awhile lost in the midst of vague musings.

I heard not thy steps as thou camest. Thine eyes were sad when they fell on me; thy voice was tired as thou spokest low—"Ah, I am a thirsty traveller." I started up from my day-dreams and poured water from my jar on thy joined palms. The leaves rustled overhead; the cuckoo sang from the unseen dark, and perfume of *babla* flowers came from the bend of the road.

I stood speechless with shame when my name thou didst ask. Indeed, what had I done for thee to keep me in remembrance? But the memory that I could give water to thee to allay thy thirst will cling to my heart and enfold it in sweetness. The morning hour is late, the bird sings in weary notes, *neem* leaves rustle overhead and I sit and think and think.

55

LANGUOR is upon your heart and the slumber is still on your eyes.

Has not the word come to you that the flower is reigning in splendour among thorns? Wake, oh awaken! Let not the time pass in vain!

At the end of the stony path, in the country of virgin solitude my

friend is sitting all alone.   Deceive
him not.   Wake, oh awaken!

What if the sky pants and trembles
with the heat of the midday sun—what
if the burning sand spreads its mantle
of thirst—

Is there no joy in the deep of your
heart?   At every footfall of yours,
will not the harp of the road break
out in sweet music of pain?

56

THUS it is that thy joy in me is so
full.   Thus it is that thou hast come
down to me.   O thou lord of all
heavens, where would be thy love if I
were not?

Thou hast taken me as thy partner
of all this wealth.   In my heart is the
endless play of thy delight.   In my life
thy will is ever taking shape.

And for this, thou who art the King

of kings hast decked thyself in beauty
to captivate my heart. And for this
thy love loses itself in the love of thy
lover, and there art thou seen in the
perfect union of two.

57

Light, my light, the world-filling light,
the eye-kissing light, heart-sweetening
light!

Ah, the light dances, my darling, at
the centre of my life; the light strikes,
my darling, the chords of my love; the
sky opens, the wind runs wild, laughter
passes over the earth.

The butterflies spread their sails on
the sea of light. Lilies and jasmines
surge up on the crest of the waves of
light.

The light is shattered into gold on
every cloud, my darling, and it scatters
gems in profusion.

Painted by Nandalal Bose

When I bring to you coloured toys

Mirth spreads from leaf to leaf, my darling, and gladness without measure. The heaven's river has drowned its banks and the flood of joy is abroad.

58

LET all the strains of joy mingle in my last song—the joy that makes the earth flow over in the riotous excess of the grass, the joy that sets the twin brothers, life and death, dancing over the wide world, the joy that sweeps in with the tempest, shaking and waking all life with laughter, the joy that sits still with its tears on the open red lotus of pain, and the joy that throws everything it has upon the dust, and knows not a word.

59

YES, I know, this is nothing but thy love, O beloved of my heart—this golden

light that dances upon the leaves, these
idle clouds sailing across the sky, this
passing breeze leaving its coolness upon
my forehead.

The morning light has flooded my
eyes—this is thy message to my heart.
Thy face is bent from above, thy eyes
look down on my eyes, and my heart
has touched thy feet.

60

ON the seashore of endless worlds
children meet. The infinite sky is
motionless overhead and the restless
water is boisterous. On the seashore
of endless worlds the children meet
with shouts and dances.

They build their houses with sand
and they play with empty shells. With
withered leaves they weave their boats
and smilingly float them on the vast

deep. Children have their play on the seashore of worlds.

They know not how to swim, they know not how to cast nets. Pearl fishers dive for pearls, merchants sail in their ships, while children gather pebbles and scatter them again. They seek not for hidden treasures, they know not how to cast nets.

The sea surges up with laughter and pale gleams the smile of the sea beach. Death-dealing waves sing meaningless ballads to the children, even like a mother while rocking her baby's cradle. The sea plays with children, and pale gleams the smile of the sea beach.

On the seashore of endless worlds children meet. Tempest roams in the pathless sky, ships get wrecked in the trackless water, death is abroad and children play. On the seashore of endless worlds is the great meeting of children.

61

THE sleep that flits on baby's eyes—
does anybody know from where it
comes? Yes, there is a rumour that
it has its dwelling where, in the fairy
village among shadows of the forest
dimly lit with glow-worms, there hang
two timid buds of enchantment. From
there it comes to kiss baby's eyes.

The smile that flickers on baby's lips
when he sleeps—does anybody know
where it was born? Yes, there is a
rumour that a young pale beam of a
crescent moon touched the edge of a
vanishing autumn cloud, and there the
smile was first born in the dream of a
dew-washed morning—the smile that
flickers on baby's lips when he sleeps.

The sweet, soft freshness that blooms
on baby's limbs—does anybody know
where it was hidden so long? Yes,
when the mother was a young girl it

lay pervading her heart in tender and silent mystery of love—the sweet, soft freshness that has bloomed on baby's limbs.

62

WHEN I bring to you coloured toys, my child, I understand why there is such a play of colours on clouds, on water, and why flowers are painted in tints—when I give coloured toys to you, my child.

When I sing to make you dance I truly know why there is music in leaves, and why waves send their chorus of voices to the heart of the listening earth—when I sing to make you dance.

When I bring sweet things to your greedy hands I know why there is honey in the cup of the flower and why fruits are secretly filled with sweet juice —when I bring sweet things to your greedy hands.

When I kiss your face to make you smile, my darling, I surely understand what the pleasure is that streams from the sky in morning light, and what delight that is which the summer breeze brings to my body—when I kiss you to make you smile.

63

Thou hast made me known to friends whom I knew not. Thou hast given me seats in homes not my own. Thou hast brought the distant near and made a brother of the stranger.

I am uneasy at heart when I have to leave my accustomed shelter; I forget that there abides the old in the new, and that there also thou abidest.

Through birth and death, in this world or in others, wherever thou leadest me it is thou, the same, the one companion of my endless life who

Painted by Surendranath Kar

On the slope of the desolate river

ever linkest my heart with bonds of
joy to the unfamiliar.

When one knows thee, then alien
there is none, then no door is shut.
Oh, grant me my prayer that I may
never lose the bliss of the touch of the
one in the play of the many.

64

ON the slope of the desolate river among
tall grasses I asked her, "Maiden, where
do you go shading your lamp with your
mantle? My house is all dark and
lonesome—lend me your light!" She
raised her dark eyes for a moment and
looked at my face through the dusk.
"I have come to the river," she said,
"to float my lamp on the stream when
the daylight wanes in the west." I
stood alone among tall grasses and
watched the timid flame of her lamp
uselessly drifting in the tide.

In the silence of gathering night I asked her, "Maiden, your lights are all lit—then where do you go with your lamp? My house is all dark and lonesome,—lend me your light." She raised her dark eyes on my face and stood for a moment doubtful. "I have come," she said at last, "to dedicate my lamp to the sky." I stood and watched her light uselessly burning in the void.

In the moonless gloom of midnight I asked her, "Maiden, what is your quest holding the lamp near your heart? My house is all dark and lonesome,—lend me your light." She stopped for a minute and thought and gazed at my face in the dark. "I have brought my light," she said, "to join the carnival of lamps." I stood and watched her little lamp uselessly lost among lights.

65

WHAT divine drink wouldst thou have, my God, from this overflowing cup of my life?

My poet, is it thy delight to see thy creation through my eyes and to stand at the portals of my ears silently to listen to thine own eternal harmony?

Thy world is weaving words in my mind and thy joy is adding music to them. Thou givest thyself to me in love and then feelest thine own entire sweetness in me.

66

SHE who ever had remained in the depth of my being, in the twilight of gleams and of glimpses; she who never opened her veils in the morning light, will be my last gift to thee, my God, folded in my final song.

Words have wooed yet failed to win
her; persuasion has stretched to her its
eager arms in vain.

I have roamed from country to
country keeping her in the core of my
heart, and around her have risen and
fallen the growth and decay of my life.

Over my thoughts and actions, my
slumbers and dreams, she reigned yet
dwelled alone and apart.

Many a man knocked at my door
and asked for her and turned away in
despair.

There was none in the world who
ever saw her face to face, and she
remained in her loneliness waiting for
thy recognition.

67

THOU art the sky and thou art the nest
as well.

O thou beautiful, there in the nest it

Painted by Nandalal Bose

Thou art the sky and thou art the nest as well

is thy love that encloses the soul with colours and sounds and odours.

There comes the morning with the golden basket in her right hand bearing the wreath of beauty, silently to crown the earth.

And there comes the evening over the lonely meadows deserted by herds, through trackless paths, carrying cool draughts of peace in her golden pitcher from the western ocean of rest.

But there, where spreads the infinite sky for the soul to take her flight in, reigns the stainless white radiance. There is no day nor night, nor form nor colour, and never, never a word.

68

THY sunbeam comes upon this earth of mine with arms outstretched and stands at my door the livelong day to carry

back to thy feet clouds made of my
tears and sighs and songs.

With fond delight thou wrappest
about thy starry breast that mantle of
misty cloud, turning it into numberless
shapes and folds and colouring it with
hues everchanging.

It is so light and so fleeting, tender
and tearful and dark, that is why thou
lovest it, O thou spotless and serene.
And that is why it may cover thy
awful white light with its pathetic
shadows.

69

THE same stream of life that runs
through my veins night and day runs
through the world and dances in
rhythmic measures.

It is the same life that shoots in joy
through the dust of the earth in
numberless blades of grass and breaks

into tumultuous waves of leaves and
flowers.

It is the same life that is rocked in
the ocean-cradle of birth and of death,
in ebb and in flow.

I feel my limbs are made glorious by
the touch of this world of life. And my
pride is from the life-throb of ages
dancing in my blood this moment.

70

Is it beyond thee to be glad with the
gladness of this rhythm? to be tossed
and lost and broken in the whirl of this
fearful joy?

All things rush on, they stop not,
they look not behind, no power can
hold them back, they rush on.

Keeping steps with that restless, rapid
music, seasons come dancing and pass
away—colours, tunes, and perfumes
pour in endless cascades in the abound-

ing joy that scatters and gives up and dies every moment.

71

THAT I should make much of myself and turn it on all sides, thus casting coloured shadows on thy radiance— such is thy *maya*.

Thou settest a barrier in thine own being and then callest thy severed self in myriad notes. This thy self-separation has taken body in me.

The poignant song is echoed through all the sky in many-coloured tears and smiles, alarms and hopes; waves rise up and sink again, dreams break and form. In me is thy own defeat of self.

This screen that thou hast raised is painted with innumerable figures with the brush of the night and the day. Behind it thy seat is woven in wondrous mysteries of curves, casting away all barren lines of straightness.

The great pageant of thee and me
has overspread the sky. With the
tune of thee and me all the air is
vibrant, and all ages pass with the hiding and seeking of thee and me.

72

HE it is, the innermost one, who
awakens my being with his deep hidden
touches.

He it is who puts his enchantment
upon these eyes and joyfully plays on
the chords of my heart in varied cadence of pleasure and pain.

He it is who weaves the web of this
maya in evanescent hues of gold and
silver, blue and green, and lets peep out
through the folds his feet, at whose
touch I forget myself.

Days come and ages pass, and it is
ever he who moves my heart in many a

name, in many a guise, in many a rapture of joy and of sorrow.

73

DELIVERANCE is not for me in renunciation. I feel the embrace of freedom in a thousand bonds of delight.

Thou ever pourest for me the fresh draught of thy wine of various colours and fragrance, filling this earthen vessel to the brim.

My world will light its hundred different lamps with thy flame and place them before the altar of thy temple.

No, I will never shut the doors of my senses. The delights of sight and hearing and touch will bear thy delight.

Yes, all my illusions will burn into illumination of joy, and all my desires ripen into fruits of love.

Painted by Abanindranath Tagore

Deliverance is not for me in renunciation.

74

THE day is no more, the shadow is upon the earth. It is time that I go to the stream to fill my pitcher.

The evening air is eager with the sad music of the water. Ah, it calls me out into the dusk. In the lonely lane there is no passer by, the wind is up, the ripples are rampant in the river.

I know not if I shall come back home. I know not whom I shall chance to meet. There at the fording in the little boat the unknown man plays upon his lute.

75

THY gifts to us mortals fulfil all our needs and yet run back to thee undiminished.

The river has its everyday work to do and hastens through fields and hamlets; yet its incessant stream winds towards the washing of thy feet.

The flower sweetens the air with its perfume; yet its last service is to offer itself to thee.

Thy worship does not impoverish the world.

From the words of the poet men take what meanings please them; yet their last meaning points to thee.

76

DAY after dAY, O lord of my life, shall I stand before thee face to face? With folded hands, O lord of all worlds, shall I stand before thee face to face?

Under thy great sky in solitude and silence, with humble heart shall I stand before thee face to face?

In this laborious world of thine, tumultuous with toil and with struggle, among hurrying crowds shall I stand before thee face to face?

And when my work shall be done in this world, O King of kings, alone and speechless shall I stand before thee face to face?

77

I KNOW thee as my God and stand apart—I do not know thee as my own and come closer. I know thee as my father and bow before thy feet—I do not grasp thy hand as my friend's.

I stand not where thou comest down and ownest thyself as mine, there to clasp thee to my heart and take thee as my comrade.

Thou art the Brother amongst my brothers, but I heed them not, I divide not my earnings with them, thus sharing my all with thee.

In pleasure and in pain I stand not

by the side of men, and thus stand
by thee. I shrink to give up my
life, and thus do not plunge into the
great waters of life.

78

WHEN the creation was new and all
the stars shone in their first splendour,
the gods held their assembly in the sky
and sang "Oh, the picture of perfection! the joy unalloyed!"

But one cried of a sudden—"It seems
that somewhere there is a break in the
chain of light and one of the stars has
been lost."

The golden string of their harp
snapped, their song stopped, and they
cried in dismay—"Yes, that lost star
was the best, she was the glory of all
heavens!"

From that day the search is un-
ceasing for her, and the cry goes on

from one to the other that in her the world has lost its one joy!

Only in the deepest silence of night the stars smile and whisper among themselves—"Vain is this seeking! Unbroken perfection is over all!"

79

IF it is not my portion to meet thee in this my life then let me ever feel that I have missed thy sight—let me not forget for a moment, let me carry the pangs of this sorrow in my dreams and in my wakeful hours.

As my days pass in the crowded market of this world and my hands grow full with the daily profits, let me ever feel that I have gained nothing — let me not forget for a moment, let me carry the pangs of this sorrow in my dreams and in my wakeful hours.

When I sit by the roadside, tired

and panting, when I spread my bed low in the dust, let me ever feel that the long journey is still before me—let me not forget for a moment, let me carry the pangs of this sorrow in my dreams and in my wakeful hours.

When my rooms have been decked out and the flutes sound and the laughter there is loud, let me ever feel that I have not invited thee to my house— let me not forget for a moment, let me carry the pangs of this sorrow in my dreams and in my wakeful hours.

80

I AM like a remnant of a cloud of autumn uselessly roaming in the sky, O my sun ever-glorious! Thy touch has not yet melted my vapour, making me one with thy light, and thus I count months and years separated from thee.

If this be thy wish and if this be thy

Painted by Nandalal Bose

I am like a remnant of a cloud

play, then take this fleeting emptiness of mine, paint it with colours, gild it with gold, float it on the wanton wind and spread it in varied wonders.

And again when it shall be thy wish to end this play at night, I shall melt and vanish away in the dark, or it may be in a smile of the white morning, in a coolness of purity transparent.

81

On many an idle day have I grieved over lost time. But it is never lost, my lord. Thou hast taken every moment of my life in thine own hands.

Hidden in the heart of things thou art nourishing seeds into sprouts, buds into blossoms, and ripening flowers into fruitfulness.

I was tired and sleeping on my idle bed and imagined all work had ceased.

In the morning I woke up and found my garden full with wonders of flowers.

82

Time is endless in thy hands, my lord. There is none to count thy minutes.

Days and nights pass and ages bloom and fade like flowers. Thou knowest how to wait.

Thy centuries follow each other perfecting a small wild flower.

We have no time to lose, and having no time we must scramble for our chances. We are too poor to be late.

And thus it is that time goes by while I give it to every querulous man who claims it, and thine altar is empty of all offerings to the last.

At the end of the day I hasten in fear lest thy gate be shut; but I find that yet there is time.

83

MOTHER, I shall weave a chain of pearls for thy neck with my tears of sorrow.

The stars have wrought their anklets of light to deck thy feet, but mine will hang upon thy breast.

Wealth and fame come from thee and it is for thee to give or to withhold them. But this my sorrow is absolutely mine own, and when I bring it to thee as my offering thou rewardest me with thy grace.

84

IT is the pang of separation that spreads throughout the world and gives birth to shapes innumerable in the infinite sky.

It is this sorrow of separation that gazes in silence all night from star to star and becomes lyric among rustling leaves in rainy darkness of July.

It is this overspreading pain that
deepens into loves and desires, into
sufferings and joys in human homes;
and this it is that ever melts and flows
in songs through my poet's heart.

85

WHEN the warriors came out first from
their master's hall, where had they hid
their power?   Where were their armour and their arms?

They looked poor and helpless, and
the arrows were showered upon them
on the day they came out from their
master's hall.

When the warriors marched back
again to their master's hall where did
they hide their power?

They had dropped the sword and
dropped the bow and the arrow; peace
was on their foreheads, and they had
left the fruits of their life behind them

on the day they marched back again to
their master's hall.

86

DEATH, thy servant, is at my door.
He has crossed the unknown sea and
brought thy call to my home.

The night is dark and my heart is
fearful—yet I will take up the lamp,
open my gates and bow to him my
welcome. It is thy messenger who
stands at my door.

I will worship him with folded hands,
and with tears. I will worship him
placing at his feet the treasure of my
heart.

He will go back with his errand done,
leaving a dark shadow on my morning;
and in my desolate home only my
forlorn self will remain as my last
offering to thee.

87

In desperate hope I go and search for her in all the corners of my room; I find her not.

My house is small and what once has gone from it can never be regained.

But infinite is thy mansion, my lord, and seeking her I have come to thy door.

I stand under the golden canopy of thine evening sky and I lift my eager eyes to thy face.

I have come to the brink of eternity from which nothing can vanish—no hope, no happiness, no vision of a face seen through tears.

Oh, dip my emptied life into that ocean, plunge it into the deepest fullness. Let me for once feel that lost sweet touch in the allness of the universe.

88

DEITY of the ruined temple! The broken strings of *Vina* sing no more your praise. The bells in the evening proclaim not your time of worship. The air is still and silent about you.

In your desolate dwelling comes the vagrant spring breeze. It brings the tidings of flowers—the flowers that for your worship are offered no more.

Your worshipper of old wanders ever longing for favour still refused. In the eventide, when fires and shadows mingle with the gloom of dust, he wearily comes back to the ruined temple with hunger in his heart.

Many a festival day comes to you in silence, deity of the ruined temple. Many a night of worship goes away with lamp unlit.

Many new images are built by masters of cunning art and carried to the holy stream of oblivion when their time is come.

Only the deity of the ruined temple remains unworshipped in deathless neglect.

89

No more noisy, loud words from me— such is my master's will. Henceforth I deal in whispers. The speech of my heart will be carried on in murmurings of a song.

Men hasten to the King's market. All the buyers and sellers are there. But I have my untimely leave in the middle of the day, in the thick of work.

Let then the flowers come out in my garden, though it is not their time; and let the midday bees strike up their lazy hum.

Full many an hour have I spent in the strife of the good and the evil, but now it is the pleasure of my playmate

of the empty days to draw my heart on
to him; and I know not why is this
sudden call to what useless incon-
sequence!

90

ON the day when death will knock at
thy door what wilt thou offer to him?

Oh, I will set before my guest the
full vessel of my life—I will never let
him go with empty hands.

All the sweet vintage of all my
autumn days and summer nights, all
the earnings and gleanings of my busy
life will I place before him at the close
of my days when death will knock at
my door.

91

O THOU the last fulfilment of life, Death,
my death, come and whisper to me!

Day after day have I kept watch for

thee; for thee have I borne the joys and pangs of life.

All that I am, that I have, that I hope and all my love have ever flowed towards thee in depth of secrecy. One final glance from thine eyes and my life will be ever thine own.

The flowers have been woven and the garland is ready for the bridegroom. After the wedding the bride shall leave her home and meet her lord alone in the solitude of night.

92

I KNOW that the day will come when my sight of this earth shall be lost, and life will take its leave in silence, drawing the last curtain over my eyes.

Yet stars will watch at night, and morning rise as before, and hours heave like sea waves casting up pleasures and pains.

When I think of this end of my moments, the barrier of the moments breaks and I see by the light of death thy world with its careless treasures. Rare is its lowliest seat, rare is its meanest of lives.

Things that I longed for in vain and things that I got—let them pass. Let me but truly possess the things that I ever spurned and overlooked.

93

I HAVE got my leave. Bid me farewell, my brothers! I bow to you all and take my departure.

Here I give back the keys of my door—and I give up all claims to my house. I only ask for last kind words from you.

We were neighbours for long, but I received more than I could give. Now the day has dawned and the lamp that lit my dark corner is out. A summons has come and I am ready for my journey.

94

At this time of my parting, wish me good luck, my friends! The sky is flushed with the dawn and my path lies beautiful

Ask not what I have with me to take there. I start on my journey with empty hands and expectant heart.

I shall put on my wedding garland. Mine is not the red-brown dress of the traveller, and though there are dangers on the way I have no fear in my mind.

The evening star will come out when my voyage is done and the plaintive notes of the twilight melodies be struck up from the King's gateway.

95

I was not aware of the moment when I first crossed the threshold of this life.

What was the power that made me open out into this vast mystery like a bud in the forest at midnight!

When in the morning I looked upon the light I felt in a moment that I was no stranger in this world, that the inscrutable without name and form had taken me in its arms in the form of my own mother.

Even so, in death the same unknown will appear as ever known to me. And because I love this life, I know I shall love death as well.

The child cries out when from the right breast the mother takes it away, in the very next moment to find in the left one its consolation.

96

WHEN I go from hence let this be my
parting word, that what I have seen is
unsurpassable.

I have tasted of the hidden honey of
this lotus that expands on the ocean of
light, and thus am I blessed—let this
be my parting word.

In this playhouse of infinite forms I
have had my play and here have I
caught sight of him that is formless.

My whole body and my limbs have
thrilled with his touch who is beyond
touch; and if the end comes here, let
it come—let this be my parting word.

97

WHEN my play was with thee I never
questioned who thou wert. I knew nor
shyness nor fear, my life was boisterous.

In the early morning thou wouldst

Drawn by Asit Kumar Haldar

When I go from hence let this be my parting word

call me from my sleep like my own comrade and lead me running from glade to glade.

On those days I never cared to know the meaning of songs thou sangest to me. Only my voice took up the tunes, and my heart danced in their cadence.

Now, when the playtime is over, what is this sudden sight that is come upon me? The world with eyes bent upon thy feet stands in awe with all its silent stars.

98

I WILL deck thee with trophies, garlands of my defeat. It is never in my power to escape unconquered.

I surely know my pride will go to the wall, my life will burst its bonds in exceeding pain, and my empty heart will sob out in music like a hollow reed, and the stone will melt in tears.

I surely know the hundred petals of

a lotus will not remain closed for ever
and the secret recess of its honey will
be bared.

From the blue sky an eye shall gaze
upon me and summon me in silence.
Nothing will be left for me, nothing
whatever, and utter death shall I re-
ceive at thy feet.

99

When I give up the helm I know that
the time has come for thee to take it.
What there is to do will be instantly
done. Vain is this struggle.

Then take away your hands and
silently put up with your defeat, my
heart, and think it your good fortune
to sit perfectly still where you are
placed.

These my lamps are blown out at
every little puff of wind, and trying to
light them I forget all else again and
again.

But I shall be wise this time and wait in the dark, spreading my mat on the floor; and whenever it is thy pleasure, my lord, come silently and take thy seat here.

100

I DIVE down into the depth of the ocean of forms, hoping to gain the perfect pearl of the formless.

No more sailing from harbour to harbour with this my weather-beaten boat. The days are long passed when my sport was to be tossed on waves.

And now I am eager to die into the deathless.

Into the audience hall by the fathomless abyss where swells up the music of toneless strings I shall take this harp of my life.

I shall tune it to the notes of for ever, and, when it has sobbed out its last

utterance, lay down my silent harp at
the feet of the silent.

101

EVER in my life have I sought thee
with my songs. It was they who led
me from door to door, and with them
have I felt about me, searching and
touching my world.

It was my songs that taught me all
the lessons I ever learnt; they showed
me secret paths, they brought before
my sight many a star on the horizon of
my heart.

They guided me all the day long to
the mysteries of the country of pleasure
and pain, and, at last, to what palace
gate have they brought me in the
evening at the end of my journey?

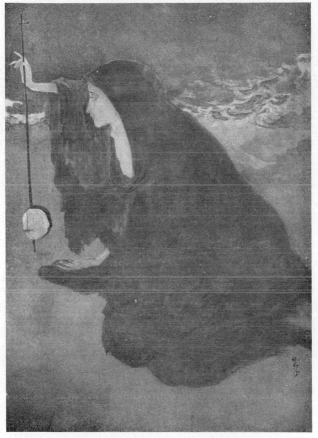

Painted by Abanindranath Tagore

Ever in my life have I sought thee with my songs

102

I BOASTED among men that I had
known you. They see your pictures in
all works of mine. They come and ask
me, "Who is he?" I know not how
to answer them. I say, "Indeed, I
cannot tell." They blame me and they
go away in scorn. And you sit there
smiling.

I put my tales of you into lasting
songs. The secret gushes out from my
heart. They come and ask me, "Tell
me all your meanings." I know not
how to answer them. I say, "Ah, who
knows what they mean!" They smile
and go away in utter scorn. And you
sit there smiling.

103

IN one salutation to thee, my God, let all my senses spread out and touch this world at thy feet.

Like a rain-cloud of July hung low with its burden of unshed showers let all my mind bend down at thy door in one salutation to thee.

Let all my songs gather together their diverse strains into a single current and flow to a sea of silence in one salutation to thee.

Like a flock of homesick cranes flying night and day back to their mountain nests let all my life take its voyage to its eternal home in one salutation to thee.

THESE translations are of poems contained in three books—Naivédya, Kheyá, and Gitánjali—to be had at the Indian Publishing House, 22 Cornwallis Street, Calcutta; and of a few poems which have appeared only in periodicals.

FRUIT–GATHERING

I

BID me and I shall gather my fruits to
bring them in full baskets into your
courtyard, though some are lost and
some not ripe.

For the season grows heavy with its
fulness, and there is a plaintive shepherd's pipe in the shade.

Bid me and I shall set sail on the
river.

The March wind is fretful, fretting
the languid waves into murmurs.

The garden has yielded its all, and
in the weary hour of evening the call
comes from your house on the shore in
the sunset.

II

My life when young was like a flower—
a flower that loosens a petal or two
from her abundance and never feels
the loss when the spring breeze comes
to beg at her door.

Now at the end of youth my life is
like a fruit, having nothing to spare,
and waiting to offer herself completely
with her full burden of sweetness.

Painted by Abanindranath Tagore

Is summer's festival only for fresh blossoms and not
also for withered leaves and faded flowers?

III

Is summer's festival only for fresh blossoms and not also for withered leaves and faded flowers?

Is the song of the sea in tune only with the rising waves?

Does it not also sing with the waves that fall?

Jewels are woven into the carpet where stands my king, but there are patient clods waiting to be touched by his feet.

Few are the wise and the great who sit by my Master, but he has taken the foolish in his arms and made me his servant for ever.

IV

I woke and found his letter with the morning.

I do not know what it says, for I cannot read.

I shall leave the wise man alone with his books, I shall not trouble him, for who knows if he can read what the letter says.

Let me hold it to my forehead and press it to my heart.

When the night grows still and stars come out one by one I will spread it on my lap and stay silent.

The rustling leaves will read it aloud to me, the rushing stream will chant it, and the seven wise stars will sing it to me from the sky.

I cannot find what I seek, I cannot understand what I would learn; but this unread letter has lightened my burdens and turned my thoughts into songs.

V

A HANDFUL of dust could hide your
signal when I did not know its meaning.

Now that I am wiser I read it in all
that hid it before.

It is painted in petals of flowers;
waves flash it from their foam; hills
hold it high on their summits.

I had my face turned from you,
therefore I read the letters awry and
knew not their meaning.

'VI

WHERE roads are made I lose my way.

In the wide water, in the blue sky there is no line of a track.

The pathway is hidden by the birds' wings, by the star-fires, by the flowers of the wayfaring seasons.

And I ask my heart if its blood carries the wisdom of the unseen way.

VII

ALAS, I cannot stay in the house, and
home has become no home to me, for
the eternal Stranger calls, he is going
along the road.

The sound of his footfall knocks at
my breast; it pains me!

The wind is up, the sea is moaning.

I leave all my cares and doubts
to follow the homeless tide, for the
Stranger calls me, he is going along
the road.

VIII

BE ready to launch forth, my heart!
and let those linger who must.

For your name has been called in the
morning sky.

Wait for none!

The desire of the bud is for the night
and dew, but the blown flower cries for
the freedom of light.

Burst your sheath, my heart, and
come forth!

IX

WHEN I lingered among my hoarded treasure I felt like a worm that feeds in the dark upon the fruit where it was born.

I leave this prison of decay.

I care not to haunt the mouldy stillness, for I go in search of everlasting youth; I throw away all that is not one with my life nor as light as my laughter.

I run through time and, O my heart, in your chariot dances the poet who sings while he wanders.

X

You took my hand and drew me to
your side, made me sit on the high seat
before all men, till I became timid,
unable to stir and walk my own way;
doubting and debating at every step
lest I should tread upon any thorn of
their disfavour.

I am freed at last!
The blow has come, the drum of
insult sounded, my seat is laid low in
the dust.
My paths are open before me.

My wings are full of the desire of
the sky.
I go to join the shooting stars of
midnight, to plunge into the profound
shadow.

I am like the storm-driven cloud of summer that, having cast off its crown of gold, hangs as a sword the thunderbolt upon a chain of lightning.

In desperate joy I run upon the dusty path of the despised; I draw near to your final welcome.

The child finds its mother when it leaves her womb.

When I am parted from you, thrown out from your household, I am free to see your face.

XI

It decks me only to mock me, this
jewelled chain of mine.

It bruises me when on my neck, it
strangles me when I struggle to tear
it off.

It grips my throat, it chokes my
singing.

Could I but offer it to your hand,
my Lord, I would be saved.

Take it from me, and in exchange
bind me to you with a garland, for I
am ashamed to stand before you with
this jewelled chain on my neck.

XII

FAR below flowed the Jumna, swift
and clear, above frowned the jutting
bank.

Hills dark with the woods and
scarred with the torrents were gathered
around.

Govinda, the great Sikh teacher,
sat on the rock reading scriptures,
when Raghunath, his disciple, proud
of his wealth, came and bowed to him
and said, "I have brought my poor
present unworthy of your acceptance."

Thus saying he displayed before the
teacher a pair of gold bangles wrought
with costly stones.

The master took up one of them,

twirling it round his finger, and the diamonds darted shafts of light.

Suddenly it slipped from his hand and rolled down the bank into the water.

"Alas," screamed Raghunath, and jumped into the stream.

The teacher set his eyes upon his book, and the water held and hid what it stole and went its way.

The daylight faded when Raghunath came back to the teacher tired and dripping.

He panted and said, "I can still get it back if you show me where it fell."

The teacher took up the remaining bangle and throwing it into the water said, "It is there."

XIII

To move is to meet you every moment,
            Fellow-traveller!
It is to sing to the falling of your
feet.
He whom your breath touches does
not glide by the shelter of the bank.
He spreads a reckless sail to the
wind and rides the turbulent water.

He who throws his doors open and
steps onward receives your greeting.
He does not stay to count his gain
or to mourn his loss; his heart beats
the drum for his march, for that is
to march with you every step,
            Fellow-traveller!

XIV

My portion of the best in this world
will come from your hands: such was
your promise.

Therefore your light glistens in my
tears.

I fear to be led by others lest I miss
you waiting in some road corner to
be my guide.

I walk my own wilful way till my
very folly tempts you to my door.

For I have your promise that my
portion of the best in this world will
come from your hands.

XV

YOUR speech is simple, my Master but not theirs who talk of you.

I understand the voice of your stars and the silence of your trees.

I know that my heart would open like a flower; that my life has filled itself at a hidden fountain.

Your songs, like birds from the lonely land of snow, are winging to build their nests in my heart against the warmth of its April, and I am content to wait for the merry season.

XVI

THEY knew the way and went to seek you along the narrow lane, but I wandered abroad into the night for I was ignorant.

I was not schooled enough to be afraid of you in the dark, therefore I came upon your doorstep unaware.

The wise rebuked me and bade me be gone, for I had not come by the lane.

I turned away in doubt, but you held me fast, and their scolding became louder every day.

XVII

I BROUGHT out my earthen lamp from my house and cried, "Come, children, I will light your path!"

The night was still dark when I returned, leaving the road to its silence, crying, "Light me, O Fire! for my earthen lamp lies broken in the dust!"

Painted by Abanindranath Tagore

I brought out my earthen lamp

XVIII

No: it is not yours to open buds into blossoms.

Shake the bud, strike it; it is beyond your power to make it blossom.

Your touch soils it, you tear its petals to pieces and strew them in the dust.

But no colours appear, and no perfume.

Ah! it is not for you to open the bud into a blossom.

He who can open the bud does it so simply.

He gives it a glance, and the life-sap stirs through its veins.

At his breath the flower spreads its wings and flutters in the wind.

Colours flush out like heart-longings, the perfume betrays a sweet secret.

He who can open the bud does it so simply.

XIX

SUDĀS, the gardener, plucked from his tank the last lotus left by the ravage of winter and went to sell it to the king at the palace gate.

There he met a traveller who said to him, "Ask your price for the last lotus, —I shall offer it to Lord Buddha."

Sudās said, "If you pay one golden *māshā* it will be yours."

The traveller paid it.

At that moment the king came out and he wished to buy the flower, for he was on his way to see Lord Buddha, and he thought, "It would be a fine thing to lay at his feet the lotus that bloomed in winter."

When the gardener said he had been

offered a golden *māshā* the king offered him ten, but the traveller doubled the price.

The gardener, being greedy, imagined a greater gain from him for whose sake they were bidding. He bowed and said, "I cannot sell this lotus."

In the hushed shade of the mango grove beyond the city wall Sudās stood before Lord Buddha, on whose lips sat the silence of love and whose eyes beamed peace like the morning star of the dew-washed autumn.

Sudās looked in his face and put the lotus at his feet and bowed his head to the dust.

Buddha smiled and asked, "What is your wish, my son?"

Sudās cried, "The least touch of your feet."

Painted by Nandalal Bose

Make me thy poet, O Night, Veiled Night

XX

MAKE me thy poet, O Night, veiled
Night!

There are some who have sat speechless for ages in thy shadow; let me
utter their songs.

Take me up on thy chariot without
wheels, running noiselessly from world
to world, thou queen in the palace of
time, thou darkly beautiful!

Many a questioning mind has
stealthily entered thy courtyard and
roamed through thy lampless house
seeking for answers.

From many a heart, pierced with
the arrow of joy from the hands of the
Unknown, have burst forth glad

chants, shaking the darkness to its foundation.

Those wakeful souls gaze in the starlight in wonder at the treasure they have suddenly found.

Make me their poet, O Night, the poet of thy fathomless silence.

XXI

I WILL meet one day the Life within me, the joy that hides in my life, though the days perplex my path with their idle dust.

I have known it in glimpses, and its fitful breath has come upon me, making my thoughts fragrant for a while.

I will meet one day the Joy without me that dwells behind the screen of light and will stand in the overflowing solitude where all things are seen as by their creator.

XXII

This autumn morning is tired with excess of light, and if your songs grow fitful and languid give me your flute awhile.

I shall but play with it as the whim takes me,—now take it on my lap, now touch it with my lips, now keep it by my side on the grass.

But in the solemn evening stillness I shall gather flowers, to deck it with wreaths, I shall fill it with fragrance; I shall worship it with the lighted lamp.

Then at night I shall come to you and give you back your flute.

You will play on it the music of midnight when the lonely crescent moon wanders among the stars.

Painted by Abanindranath Tagore

This autumn morning is tired with excess of light

XXIII

THE poet's mind floats and dances on the waves of life amidst the voices of wind and water.

Now when the sun has set and the darkened sky draws upon the sea like drooping lashes upon a weary eye it is time to take away his pen, and let his thoughts sink into the bottom of the deep amid the eternal secret of that silence.

XXIV

THE night is dark and your slumber is deep in the hush of my being.

Wake, O Pain of Love, for I know not how to open the door, and I stand outside.

The hours wait, the stars watch, the wind is still, the silence is heavy in my heart.

Wake, Love, wake! brim my empty cup, and with a breath of song ruffle the night.

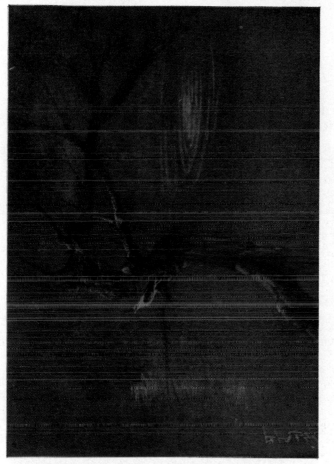

Painted by Abanindranath Tagore

The bird of the morning sings

XXV

The bird of the morning sings.

Whence has he word of the morning before the morning breaks, and when the dragon night still holds the sky in its cold black coils?

Tell me, bird of the morning, how, through the twofold night of the sky and the leaves, he found his way into your dream, the messenger out of the east?

The world did not believe you when you cried, "The sun is on his way, the night is no more."

O sleeper, awake!

Bare your forehead, waiting for the first blessing of light, and sing with the bird of the morning in glad faith.

XXVI

THE beggar in me lifted his lean hands to the starless sky and cried into night's ear with his hungry voice.

His prayers were to the blind Darkness who lay like a fallen god in a desolate heaven of lost hopes.

The cry of desire eddied round a chasm of despair, a wailing bird circling its empty nest.

But when morning dropped anchor at the rim of the East, the beggar in me leapt and cried:

"Blessed am I that the deaf night denied me—that its coffer was empty."

He cried, "O Life, O Light, you are precious! and precious is the joy that at last has known you!"

XXVII

SANĀTAN was telling his beads by the Ganges when a Brahmin in rags came to him and said, "Help me, I am poor!"

"My alms-bowl is all that is my own," said Sanātan, "I have given away everything I had."

"But my lord Shiva came to me in my dreams," said the Brahmin, "and counselled me to come to you."

Sanātan suddenly remembered he had picked up a stone without price among the pebbles on the river-bank, and thinking that some one might need it hid it in the sands.

He pointed out the spot to the Brahmin, who wondering dug up the stone.

The Brahmin sat on the earth and mused alone till the sun went down behind the trees, and cowherds went home with their cattle.

Then he rose and came slowly to Sanātan and said, "Master, give me the least fraction of the wealth that disdains all the wealth of the world."

And he threw the precious stone into the water.

XXVIII

TIME after time I came to your gate
with raised hands, asking for more and
yet more.

You gave and gave, now in slow
measure, now in sudden excess.

I took some, and some things I let
drop; some lay heavy on my hands;
some I made into playthings and broke
them when tired; till the wrecks and
the hoard of your gifts grew immense,
hiding you, and the ceaseless expecta-
tion wore my heart out.

Take, oh take—has now become my
cry.

Shatter all from this beggar's bowl:
put out this lamp of the importunate
watcher: hold my hands, raise me from
the still gathering heap of your gifts
into the bare infinity of your uncrowded
presence.

XXIX

You have set me among those who are defeated.

I know it is not for me to win, nor to leave the game.

I shall plunge into the pool although but to sink to the bottom.

I shall play the game of my undoing.

I shall stake all I have and when I lose my last penny I shall stake myself, and then I think I shall have won through my utter defeat.

Painted by Nobendranath Tagore

A smile of mirth spread over the sky

XXX

A SMILE of mirth spread over the sky
when you dressed my heart in rags and
sent her forth into the road to beg.

She went from door to door, and
many a time when her bowl was nearly
full she was robbed.

At the end of the weary day she
came to your palace gate holding up
her pitiful bowl, and you came and
took her hand and seated her beside
you on your throne.

XXXI

"Who among you will take up the duty of feeding the hungry?" Lord Buddha asked his followers when famine raged at Shravasti.

Ratnākar, the banker, hung his head and said, "Much more is needed than all my wealth to feed the hungry."

Jaysen, the chief of the King's army, said, "I would gladly give my life's blood, but there is not enough food in my house."

Dharmapāl, who owned broad acres of land, said with a sigh, "The drought demon has sucked my fields dry. I know not how to pay King's dues."

Then rose Supriyā, the mendicant's daughter.

She bowed to all and meekly said, "I will feed the hungry."

"How!" they cried in surprise. "How can you hope to fulfil that vow?"

"I am the poorest of you all," said Supriyā, "that is my strength. I have my coffer and my store at each of your houses."

XXXII

My king was unknown to me, therefore when he claimed his tribute I was bold to think I would hide myself leaving my debts unpaid.

I fled and fled behind my day's work and my night's dreams.

But his claims followed me at every breath I drew.

Thus I came to know that I am known to him and no place left which is mine.

Now I wish to lay my all before his feet, and gain the right to my place in his kingdom.

XXXIII

When I thought I would mould you, an image from my life for men to worship, I brought my dust and desires and all my coloured delusions and dreams.

When I asked you to mould with my life an image from your heart for you to love, you brought your fire and force, and truth, loveliness and peace.

XXXIV

"Sire," announced the servant to the King, "the saint Narottam has never deigned to enter your royal temple.

"He is singing God's praise under the trees by the open road.   The temple is empty of worshippers.

"They flock round him like bees round the white lotus, leaving the golden jar of honey unheeded."

The King, vexed at heart, went to the spot where Narottam sat on the grass.

He asked him, "Father, why leave my temple of the golden dome and sit on the dust outside to preach God's love?"

"Because God is not there in your temple," said Narottam.

The King frowned and said, "Do you know, twenty millions of gold went to the making of that marvel of art, and it was consecrated to God with costly rites?"

"Yes, I know it," answered Narottam. "It was in that year when thousands of your people whose houses had been burned stood vainly asking for help at your door.

"And God said, 'The poor creature who can give no shelter to his brothers would build my house!'

"And he took his place with the shelterless under the trees by the road.

"And that golden bubble is empty of all but hot vapour of pride."

The King cried in anger, "Leave my land."

Calmly said the saint, "Yes, banish me where you have banished my God."

XXXV

THE trumpet lies in the dust.
 The wind is weary, the light is dead.
 Ah, the evil day!
 Come, fighters, carrying your flags,
and singers, with your war-songs!
 Come, pilgrims of the march, hurry-
ing on your journey!
 The trumpet lies in the dust waiting
for us.

 I was on my way to the temple with
my evening offerings, seeking for a
place of rest after the day's dusty toil:
hoping my hurts would be healed and
the stains in my garment washed
white, when I found thy trumpet lying
in the dust.
 Was it not the hour for me to light
my evening lamp?

Painted by Abanindranath Tagore

The trumpet lies in the dust

Had not the night sung its lullaby to the stars?

O thou blood-red rose, my poppies of sleep have paled and faded!

I was certain my wanderings were over and my debts all paid when suddenly I came upon thy trumpet lying in the dust.

Strike my drowsy heart with thy spell of youth!

Let my joy in life blaze up in fire.

Let the shafts of awakening fly through the heart of night, and a thrill of dread shake blindness and palsy.

I have come to raise thy trumpet from the dust.

Sleep is no more for me—my walk shall be through showers of arrows.

Some shall run out of their houses and come to my side—some shall weep.

Some in their beds shall toss and groan in dire dreams.

For to-night thy trumpet shall be sounded.

From thee I have asked peace only to find shame.

Now I stand before thee—help me to put on my armour!

Let hard blows of trouble strike fire into my life.

Let my heart beat in pain, the drum of thy victory.

My hands shall be utterly emptied to take up thy trumpet.

XXXVI

WHEN, mad in their mirth, they raised dust to soil thy robe, O Beautiful, it made my heart sick.

I cried to thee and said, "Take thy rod of punishment and judge them."

The morning light struck upon those eyes, red with the revel of night; the place of the white lily greeted their burning breath; the stars through the depth of the sacred dark stared at their carousing   at those that raised dust to soil thy robe, O Beautiful!

Thy judgment seat was in the flower garden, in the birds' notes in springtime: in the shady river-banks, where the trees muttered in answer to the muttering of the waves.

O my Lover, they were pitiless in their passion.

They prowled in the dark to snatch thy ornaments to deck their own desires.

When they had struck thee and thou wert pained, it pierced me to the quick, and I cried to thee and said, "Take thy sword, O my Lover, and judge them!"

Ah, but thy justice was vigilant.

A mother's tears were shed on their insolence; the imperishable faith of a lover hid their spears of rebellion in its own wounds.

Thy judgment was in the mute pain of sleepless love: in the blush of the chaste: in the tears of the night of the desolate: in the pale morning-light of forgiveness.

O Terrible, they in their reckless greed climbed thy gate at night, breaking into thy storehouse to rob thee.

But the weight of their plunder grew

immense, too heavy to carry or to remove.

Thereupon I cried to thee and said,
Forgive them, O Terrible!

Thy forgiveness burst in storms,
throwing them down, scattering their
thefts in the dust.

Thy forgiveness was in the thunder-
stone; in the shower of blood; in the
angry red of the sunset.

XXXVII

Upagupta, the disciple of Buddha, lay asleep on the dust by the city wall of Mathura.

Lamps were all out, doors were all shut, and stars were all hidden by the murky sky of August.

Whose feet were those tinkling with anklets, touching his breast of a sudden?

He woke up startled, and the light from a woman's lamp struck his forgiving eyes.

It was the dancing girl, starred with jewels, clouded with a pale-blue mantle, drunk with the wine of her youth.

She lowered her lamp and saw the young face, austerely beautiful.

"Forgive me, young ascetic," said

the woman; "graciously come to my
house.   The dusty earth is not a fit bed
for you."

The ascetic answered, "Woman, go
on your way; when the time is ripe I
will come to you."

Suddenly the black night showed its
teeth in a flash of lightning.

The storm growled from the corner
of the sky, and the woman trembled in
fear.

.   .   .   .   .   .

The branches of the wayside trees
were aching with blossom.

Gay notes of the flute came floating
in the warm spring air from afar.

The citizens had gone to the woods,
to the festival of flowers.

From the mid-sky gazed the full
moon on the shadows of the silent
town.

The young ascetic was walking in the lonely street, while overhead the lovesick *koels* urged from the mango branches their sleepless plaint.

Upagupta passed through the city gates, and stood at the base of the rampart.

What woman lay in the shadow of the wall at his feet, struck with the black pestilence, her body spotted with sores, hurriedly driven away from the town?

The ascetic sat by her side, taking her head on his knees, and moistened her lips with water and smeared her body with balm.

"Who are you, merciful one?" asked the woman.

"The time, at last, has come to visit you, and I am here," replied the young ascetic.

XXXVIII

THIS is no mere dallying of love between us, my lover.

Again and again have swooped down upon me the screaming nights of storm, blowing out my lamp: dark doubts have gathered, blotting out all stars from my sky.

Again and again the banks have burst, letting the flood sweep away my harvest, and wailing and despair have rent my sky from end to end.

This have I learnt that there are blows of pain in your love, never the cold apathy of death.

XXXIX

THE wall breaks asunder, light, like divine laughter, bursts in.

Victory, O Light!

The heart of the night is pierced!

With your flashing sword cut in twain the tangle of doubt and feeble desires!

Victory!

Come, Implacable!

Come, you who are terrible in your whiteness.

O Light, your drum sounds in the march of fire, and the red torch is held on high; death dies in a burst of splendour!

Painted by Nobendranath Tagore

The wall breaks asunder, light, like divine laughter, bursts in

XL

O FIRE, my brother, I sing victory to you.

You are the bright red image of fearful freedom.

You swing your arms in the sky, you sweep your impetuous fingers across the harp-string, your dance music is beautiful.

When my days are ended and the gates are opened you will burn to ashes this cordage of hands and feet.

My body will be one with you, my heart will be caught in the whirls of your frenzy, and the burning heat that was my life will flash up and mingle itself in your flame.

XLI

THE Boatman is out crossing the wild sea at night.

The mast is aching because of its full sails filled with the violent wind.

Stung with the night's fang the sky falls upon the sea, poisoned with black fear.

The waves dash their heads against the dark unseen, and the Boatman is out crossing the wild sea.

The Boatman is out, I know not for what tryst, startling the night with the sudden white of his sails.

I know not at what shore, at last, he lands to reach the silent courtyard where the lamp is burning and to find her who sits in the dust and waits.

What is the quest that makes his boat care not for storm nor darkness?

Is it heavy with gems and pearls?

Ah, no, the Boatman brings with him no treasure, but only a white rose in his hand and a song on his lips.

It is for her who watches alone at night with her lamp burning.

She dwells in the wayside hut.

Her loose hair flies in the wind and hides her eyes.

The storm shrieks through her broken doors, the light flickers in her earthen lamp flinging shadows on the walls.

Through the howl of the winds she hears him call her name, she whose name is unknown.

It is long since the Boatman sailed.

It will be long before the day breaks and he knocks at the door.

The drums will not be beaten and none will know.

Only light shall fill the house, blessed shall be the dust, and the heart glad.

All doubts shall vanish in silence when the Boatman comes to the shore.

Painted by Nandalal Bose

I cling to this living raft, my body

XLII

I CLING to this living raft, my body, in the narrow stream of my earthly years. I leave it when the crossing is over.

And then?

I do not know if the light there and the darkness are the same.

The Unknown is the perpetual freedom:

He is pitiless in his love.

He crushes the shell for the pearl, dumb in the prison of the dark.

You muse and weep for the days that are done, poor heart!

Be glad that days are to come!

The hour strikes, O pilgrim!

It is time for you to take the parting of the ways!

His face will be unveiled once again and you shall meet.

XLIII

OVER the relic of Lord Buddha King Bimbisār built a shrine, a salutation in white marble.

There in the evening would come all the brides and daughters of the King's house to offer flowers and light lamps.

When the son became king in his time he washed his father's creed away with blood, and lit sacrificial fires with its sacred books.

The autumn day was dying.
The evening hour of worship was near.
Shrimati, the queen's maid, devoted to Lord Buddha, having bathed in holy water, and decked the golden tray with

lamps and fresh white blossoms, silently raised her dark eyes to the queen's face.

The queen shuddered in fear and said, "Do you not know, foolish girl, that death is the penalty for whoever brings worship to Buddha's shrine?

"Such is the king's will."

Shrimati bowed to the queen, and turning away from her door came and stood before Amitā, the newly wed bride of the king's son.

A mirror of burnished gold on her lap, the newly wed bride was braiding her dark long tresses and painting the red spot of good luck at the parting of her hair.

Her hands trembled when she saw the young maid, and she cried, "What fearful peril would you bring me! Leave me this instant."

Princess Shuklā sat at the window reading her book of romance by the light of the setting sun.

She started when she saw at her door the maid with the sacred offerings.

Her book fell down from her lap, and she whispered in Shrimati's ears, "Rush not to death, daring woman!"

Shrimati walked from door to door.

She raised her head and cried, "O women of the king's house, hasten!

"The time for our Lord's worship is come!"

Some shut their doors in her face and some reviled her.

The last gleam of daylight faded from the bronze dome of the palace tower.

Deep shadows settled in street corners: the bustle of the city was hushed: the gong at the temple of Shiva announced the time of the evening prayer.

In the dark of the autumn evening, deep as a limpid lake, stars throbbed with light, when the guards of the palace garden were startled to see through the trees a row of lamps burning at the shrine of Buddha.

They ran with their swords unsheathed, crying, "Who are you, foolish one, reckless of death?"

"I am Shrimati," replied a sweet voice, "the servant of Lord Buddha."

The next moment her heart's blood coloured the cold marble with its red.

And in the still hour of stars died the light of the last lamp of worship at the foot of the shrine.

XLIV

THE day that stands between you and me makes her last bow of farewell.

The night draws her veil over her face, and hides the one lamp burning in my chamber.

Your dark servant comes noiselessly and spreads the bridal carpet for you to take your seat there alone with me in the wordless silence till night is done.

XLV

My night has passed on the bed of sorrow, and my eyes are tired. My heavy heart is not yet ready to meet morning with its crowded joys.

Draw a veil over this naked light, beckon aside from me this glaring flash and dance of life.

Let the mantle of tender darkness cover me in its folds, and cover my pain awhile from the pressure of the world.

XLVI

THE time is past when I could repay
her for all that I received.

Her night has found its morning and
thou hast taken her to thy arms: and
to thee I bring my gratitude and my
gifts that were for her.

For all hurts and offences to her I
come to thee for forgiveness.

I offer to thy service those flowers
of my love that remained in bud when
she waited for them to open.

XLVII

I FOUND a few old letters of mine
carefully hidden in her box—a few
small toys for her memory to play with.

With a timorous heart she tried to
steal these trifles from time's turbulent
stream, and said, "These are mine
only!"

Ah, there is no one now to claim
them, who can pay their price with
loving care, yet here they are still.

Surely there is love in this world to
save her from utter loss, even like this
love of hers that saved these letters
with such fond care.

XLVIII

Bring beauty and order into my forlorn life, woman, as you brought them into my house when you lived.

Sweep away the dusty fragments of the hours, fill the empty jars, and mend all that has been neglected.

Then open the inner door of the shrine, light the candle, and let us meet there in silence before our God.

Painted by Abanindranath Tagore

The pain was great when the strings were being
tuned, my Master!

XLIX

THE pain was great when the strings
were being tuned, my Master!
 Begin your music, and let me forget
the pain; let me feel in beauty what
you had in your mind through those
pitiless days.

 The waning night lingers at my
doors, let her take her leave in songs.
 Pour your heart into my life strings,
my Master, in tunes that descend from
your stars.

L

In the lightning flash of a moment
I have seen the immensity of your
creation in my life—creation through
many a death from world to world.

I weep at my unworthiness when I
see my life in the hands of the unmeaning hours,—but when I see it in your
hands I know it is too precious to be
squandered among shadows.

LI

I KNOW that at the dim end of some day the sun will bid me its farewell.

Shepherds will play their pipes beneath the banyan trees, and cattle graze on the slope by the river, while my days will pass into the dark.

This is my prayer, that I may know before I leave why the earth called me to her arms.

Why her night's silence spoke to me of stars, and her daylight kissed my thoughts into flower.

Before I go may I linger over my last refrain, completing its music, may the lamp be lit to see your face and the wreath woven to crown you.

LII

WHAT music is that in whose measure the world is rocked?

We laugh when it beats upon the crest of life, we shrink in terror when it returns into the dark.

But the play is the same that comes and goes with the rhythm of the endless music.

You hide your treasure in the palm of your hand, and we cry that we are robbed.

But open and shut your palm as you will, the gain and the loss are the same.

At the game you play with your own self you lose and win at once.

LIII

I HAVE kissed this world with my eyes and my limbs; I have wrapt it within my heart in numberless folds; I have flooded its days and nights with thoughts till the world and my life have grown one,—and I love my life because I love the light of the sky so enwoven with me.

If to leave this world be as real as to love it—then there must be a meaning in the meeting and the parting of life.

If that love were deceived in death, then the canker of this deceit would eat into all things, and the stars would shrivel and grow black.

LIV

The Cloud said to me, "I vanish"; the Night said, "I plunge into the fiery dawn."

The Pain said, "I remain in deep silence as his footprint."

"I die into the fulness," said my life to me.

The Earth said, "My lights kiss your thoughts every moment."

"The days pass," Love said, "but I wait for you."

Death said, "I ply the boat of your life across the sea."

LV

TULSIDAS, the poet, was wandering, deep in thought, by the Ganges, in that lonely spot where they burn their dead.

He found a woman sitting at the feet of the corpse of her dead husband, gaily dressed as for a wedding.

She rose as she saw him, bowed to him, and said, "Permit me, Master, with your blessing, to follow my husband to heaven."

"Why such hurry, my daughter?" asked Tulsidas. "Is not this earth also His who made heaven?"

"For heaven I do not long," said the woman. "I want my husband."

Tulsidas smiled and said to her, "Go back to your home, my child. Before the month is over you will find your husband."

The woman went back with glad hope.   Tulsidas came to her every day and gave her high thoughts to think, till her heart was filled to the brim with divine love.

When the month was scarcely over, her neighbours came to her, asking, "Woman, have you found your husband?"

The widow smiled and said, "I have."

Eagerly they asked, "Where is he?"

"In my heart is my lord, one with me," said the woman.

LVI

You came for a moment to my side and touched me with the great mystery of the woman that there is in the heart of creation.

She who is ever returning to God his own outflowing of sweetness; she is the ever fresh beauty and youth in nature; she dances in the bubbling streams and sings in the morning light; she with heaving waves suckles the thirsty earth; in her the Eternal One breaks in two in a joy that no longer may contain itself, and overflows in the pain of love.

LVII

Who is she who dwells in my heart,
the woman forlorn for ever?

I wooed her and I failed to win her.

I decked her with wreaths and sang
in her praise.

A smile shone in her face for a moment, then it faded.

"I have no joy in thee," she cried,
the woman in sorrow.

I bought her jewelled anklets and
fanned her with a fan gem-studded; I
made her a bed on a bedstead of gold.

There flickered a gleam of gladness
in her eyes, then it died.

"I have no joy in these," she cried,
the woman in sorrow.

I seated her upon a car of triumph

and drove her from end to end of the earth.

Conquered hearts bowed down at her feet, and shouts of applause rang in the sky.

Pride shone in her eyes for a moment, then it was dimmed in tears.

"I have no joy in conquest," she cried, the woman in sorrow.

I asked her, "Tell me whom do you seek?"

She only said, "I wait for him of the unknown name."

Days pass by and she cries, "When will my beloved come whom I know not, and be known to me for ever?"

LVIII

Yours is the light that breaks forth
from the dark, and the good that
sprouts from the cleft heart of strife.

Yours is the house that opens upon
the world, and the love that calls to
the battlefield.

Yours is the gift that still is a gain
when everything is a loss, and the life
that flows through the caverns of
death.

Yours is the heaven that lies in the
common dust, and you are there for
me, you are there for all.

LIX

WHEN the weariness of the road is upon me, and the thirst of the sultry day; when the ghostly hours of the dusk throw their shadows across my life, then I cry not for your voice only, my friend, but for your touch.

There is an anguish in my heart for the burden of its riches not given to you.

Put out your hand through the night, let me hold it and fill it and keep it; let me feel its touch along the lengthening stretch of my loneliness.

LX

The odour cries in the bud, "Ah me, the day departs, the happy day of spring, and I am a prisoner in petals!"

Do not lose heart, timid thing!

Your bonds will burst, the bud will open into flower, and when you die in the fulness of life, even then the spring will live on.

The odour pants and flutters within the bud, crying, "Ah me, the hours pass by, yet I do not know where I go, or what it is I seek!"

Do not lose heart, timid thing!

The spring breeze has overheard your desire, the day will not end before you have fulfilled your being.

Dark is the future to her, and the

odour cries in despair, "Ah me, through whose fault is my life so unmeaning?

"Who can tell me, why I am at all?"

Do not lose heart, timid thing!

The perfect dawn is near when you will mingle your life with all life and know at last your purpose.

LXI

She is still a child, my lord.

She runs about your palace and plays, and tries to make of you a plaything as well.

She heeds not when her hair tumbles down and her careless garment drags in the dust.

She falls asleep when you speak to her and answers not—and the flower you give her in the morning slips to the dust from her hands.

When the storm bursts and darkness is over the sky she is sleepless; her dolls lie scattered on the earth and she clings to you in terror.

She is afraid that she may fail in service to you.

But with a smile you watch her at her game.

Painted by Nandalal Bose

She is still a child

You know her.

The child sitting in the dust is your destined bride; her play will be stilled and deepened into love.

LXII

"Wʜᴀᴛ is there but the sky, O Sun, that can hold thine image?"

"I dream of thee, but to serve thee I can never hope," the dewdrop wept and said, "I am too small to take thee unto me, great lord, and my life is all tears."

"I illumine the limitless sky, yet I can yield myself up to a tiny drop of dew," thus the Sun said; "I shall become but a sparkle of light and fill you, and your little life will be a laughing orb."

LXIII

NOT for me is the love that knows no restraint, but like the foaming wine that having burst its vessel in a moment would run to waste.

Send me the love which is cool and pure like your rain that blesses the thirsty earth and fills the homely earthen jars.

Send me the love that would soak down into the centre of being, and from there would spread like the unseen sap through the branching tree of life, giving birth to fruits and flowers.

Send me the love that keeps the heart still with the fulness of peace.

LXIV

THE sun had set on the western margin of the river among the tangle of the forest.

The hermit boys had brought the cattle home, and sat round the fire to listen to the master, Guatama, when a strange boy came, and greeted him with fruits and flowers, and, bowing low at his feet, spoke in a bird-like voice—"Lord, I have come to thee to be taken into the path of the supreme Truth.

"My name is Satyakāma."

"Blessings be on thy head," said the master.

"Of what clan art thou, my child? It is only fitting for a Brahmin to aspire to the highest wisdom."

"Master," answered the boy, "I know not of what clan I am. I shall go and ask my mother."

Thus saying, Satyakāma took leave, and wading across the shallow stream, came back to his mother's hut, which stood at the end of the sandy waste at the edge of the sleeping village.

The lamp burnt dimly in the room, and the mother stood at the door in the dark waiting for her son's return.

She clasped him to her bosom, kissed him on his hair, and asked him of his errand to the master.

"What is the name of my father, dear mother?" asked the boy.

"It is only fitting for a Brahmin to aspire to the highest wisdom, said Lord Guatama to me."

The woman lowered her eyes, and spoke in a whisper.

"In my youth I was poor and had many masters. Thou didst come to thy mother Jabālā's arms, my darling, who had no husband."

The early rays of the sun glistened on the tree-tops of the forest hermitage.

The students, with their tangled hair still wet with their morning bath, sat under the ancient tree, before the master.

There came Satyakāma.

He bowed low at the feet of the sage, and stood silent.

"Tell me," the great teacher asked him, "of what clan art thou?"

"My lord," he answered, "I know it not. My mother said when I asked her, 'I had served many masters in my youth, and thou hadst come to thy mother Jabālā's arms, who had no husband.'"

There rose a murmur like the angry hum of bees disturbed in their hive; and the students muttered at the shameless insolence of that outcast.

Master Guatama rose from his seat, stretched out his arms, took the boy to his bosom, and said, "Best of all Brahmins art thou, my child. Thou hast the noblest heritage of truth."

LXV

MAY be there is one house in this city
where the gate opens for ever this
morning at the touch of the sunrise,
where the errand of the light is fulfilled.

The flowers have opened in hedges
and gardens, and may be there is one
heart that has found in them this
morning the gift that has been on its
voyage from endless time.

Painted by Abanindranath Tagore

Maybe there is one house in this city

LXVI

LISTEN, my heart, in his flute is the music of the smell of wild flowers, of the glistening leaves and gleaming water, of shadows resonant with bees' wings.

The flute steals his smile from my friend's lips and spreads it over my life.

LXVII

You always stand alone beyond the stream of my songs.

The waves of my tunes wash your feet but I know not how to reach them.

This play of mine with you is a play from afar.

It is the pain of separation that melts into melody through my flute.

I wait for the time when your boat crosses over to my shore and you take my flute into your own hands.

LXVIII

SUDDENLY the window of my heart
flew open this morning, the window
that looks out on your heart.

I wondered to see that the name by
which you know me is written in April
leaves and flowers, and I sat silent.

The curtain was blown away for a
moment between my songs and yours.

I found that your morning light was
full of my own mute songs unsung; I
thought that I would learn them at
your feet—and I sat silent.

LXIX

You were in the centre of my heart, therefore when my heart wandered she never found you; you hid yourself from my loves and hopes till the last, for you were always in them.

You were the inmost joy in the play of my youth, and when I was too busy with the play the joy was passed by.

You sang to me in the ecstasies of my life and I forgot to sing to you.

LXX

WHEN you hold your lamp in the sky it throws its light on my face and its shadow falls over you.

When I hold the lamp of love in my heart its light falls on you and I am left standing behind in the shadow.

LXXI

O THE waves, the sky-devouring waves, glistening with light, dancing with life, the waves of eddying joy, rushing for ever.

The stars rock upon them, thoughts of every tint are cast up out of the deep and scattered on the beach of life.
Birth and death rise and fall with their rhythm, and the sea-gull of my heart spreads its wings crying in delight.

Painted by Nandalal Bose

O, the Waves, the Sky-devouring Waves!

LXXII

THE joy ran from all the world to build my body.

The lights of the skies kissed and kissed her till she woke.

Flowers of hurrying summers sighed in her breath and voices of winds and water sang in her movements.

The passion of the tide of colours in clouds and in forests flowed into her life, and the music of all things caressed her limbs into shape.

She is my bride,—she has lighted her lamp in my house.

LXXIII

THE spring with its leaves and flowers
has come into my body.

The bees hum there the morning
long, and the winds idly play with the
shadows.

A sweet fountain springs up from
the heart of my heart.

My eyes are washed with delight
like the dew-bathed morning, and life
is quivering in all my limbs like the
sounding strings of the lute.

Are you wandering alone by the
shore of my life, where the tide is in
flood, O lover of my endless days?

Are my dreams flitting round you
like the moths with their many-coloured wings?

And are those your songs that are echoing in the dark caves of my being?

Who but you can hear the hum of the crowded hours that sounds in my veins to-day, the glad steps that dance in my breast, the clamour of the restless life beating its wings in my body?

LXXIV

My bonds are cut, my debts are paid,
my door has been opened, I go every-
where.

They crouch in their corner and
weave their web of pale hours, they
count their coins sitting in the dust
and call me back.

But my sword is forged, my armour
is put on, my horse is eager to run.
I shall win my kingdom.

Painted by Surendranath Kar

The spring with its leaves and flowers has come into
my body

LXXV

It was only the other day that I came to your earth, naked and nameless, with a wailing cry.

To-day my voice is glad, while you, my lord, stand aside to make room that I may fill my life.

Even when I bring you my songs for an offering I have the secret hope that men will come and love me for them.

You love to discover that I love this world where you have brought me.

LXXVI

Timidly I cowered in the shadow of safety, but now, when the surge of joy carries my heart upon its crest, my heart clings to the cruel rock of its trouble.

I sat alone in a corner of my house thinking it too narrow for any guest, but now when its door is flung open by an unbidden joy I find there is room for thee and for all the world.

I walked upon tiptoe, careful of my person, perfumed, and adorned—but now when a glad whirlwind has overthrown me in the dust I laugh and roll on the earth at thy feet like a child.

LXXVII

THE world is yours at once and for ever.

And because you have no want, my king, you have no pleasure in your wealth.

It is as though it were naught.

Therefore through slow time you give me what is yours, and ceaselessly win your kingdom in me.

Day after day you buy your sunrise from my heart, and you find your love carven into the image of my life.

LXXVIII

To the birds you gave songs, the birds
gave you songs in return.

You gave me only voice, yet asked
for more, and I sing.

You made your winds light and they
are fleet in their service. You bur-
dened my hands that I myself may
lighten them, and at last, gain unbur-
dened freedom for your service.

You created your Earth filling its
shadows with fragments of light.

There you paused; you left me
empty-handed in the dust to create
your heaven.

To all things else you give; from me
you ask.

The harvest of my life ripens in the
sun and the shower till I reap more
than you sowed, gladdening your heart,
O Master of the golden granary.

LXXIX

LET me not pray to be sheltered from dangers but to be fearless in facing them.

Let me not beg for the stilling of my pain but for the heart to conquer it.

Let me not look for allies in life's battlefield but to my own strength.

Let me not crave in anxious fear to be saved but hope for the patience to win my freedom.

Grant me that I may not be a coward, feeling your mercy in my success alone; but let me find the grasp of your hand in my failure.

LXXX

You did not know yourself when you
dwelt alone, and there was no crying
of an errand when the wind ran from
the hither to the farther shore.

I came and you woke, and the skies
blossomed with lights.
You made me open in many flowers;
rocked me in the cradles of many forms;
hid me in death and found me again in
life.

I came and your heart heaved; pain
came to you and joy.
You touched me and tingled into
love.

But in my eyes there is a film of
shame and in my breast a flicker of

fear; my face is veiled and I weep when I cannot see you.

Yet I know the endless thirst in your heart for sight of me, the thirst that cries at my door in the repeated knockings of sunrise.

LXXXI

You, in your timeless watch, listen to my approaching steps while your gladness gathers in the morning twilight and breaks in the burst of light.

The nearer I draw to you the deeper grows the fervour in the dance of the sea.

Your world is a branching spray of light filling your hands, but your heaven is in my secret heart; it slowly opens its buds in shy love.

LXXXII

I WILL utter your name, sitting alone among the shadows of my silent thoughts.

I will utter it without words, I will utter it without purpose.

For I am like a child that calls its mother an hundred times, glad that it can say "Mother."

LXXXIII

I

I FEEL that all the stars shine in me.

The world breaks into my life like a flood.

The flowers blossom in my body.

All the youthfulness of land and water smokes like an incense in my heart; and the breath of all things plays on my thoughts as on a flute.

II

When the world sleeps I come to your door.

The stars are silent, and I am afraid to sing.

I wait and watch, till your shadow

passes by the balcony of night and I return with a full heart.

Then in the morning I sing by the roadside;

The flowers in the hedge give me answer and the morning air listens,

The travellers suddenly stop and look in my face, thinking I have called them by their names.

III

Keep me at your door ever attending to your wishes, and let me go about in your Kingdom accepting your call.

Let me not sink and disappear in the depth of languor.

Let not my life be worn out to tatters by penury of waste.

Let not those doubts encompass me, —the dust of distractions.

Let me not pursue many paths to gather many things.

Let me not bend my heart to the yoke of the many.

Let me hold my head high in the courage and pride of being your servant.

LXXXIV

THE OARSMEN

Do you hear the tumult of death afar,
The call midst the fire-floods and
    poisonous clouds
—The Captain's call to the steersman
    to turn the ship to an unnamed
    shore,
For that time is over—the stagnant
    time in the port—
Where the same old merchandise is
    bought and sold in an endless
    round,
Where dead things drift in the ex-
    haustion and emptiness of truth.

They wake up in sudden fear and ask,
    "Comrades, what hour has struck?
When shall the dawn begin?"

The clouds have blotted away the
stars—
Who is there then can see the beckon-
ing finger of the day?
They run out with oars in hand, the
beds are emptied, the mother
prays, the wife watches by the
door;
There is a wail of parting that rises to
the sky,
And there is the Captain's voice in
the dark:
"Come, sailors, for the time in the
harbour is over!"

All the black evils in the world have
overflowed their banks,
Yet, oarsmen, take your places with
the blessing of sorrow in your
souls!
Whom do you blame, brothers? Bow
your heads down!
The sin has been yours and ours.

The heat growing in the heart of God
    for ages—
The cowardice of the weak, the arro-
    gance of the strong, the greed of
    fat prosperity, the rancour of the
    wronged, pride of race, and insult
    to man—
Has burst God's peace, raging in storm.

Like a ripe pod, let the tempest break
    its heart into pieces, scattering
    thunders.
Stop your bluster of dispraise and of
    self-praise,
And with the calm of silent prayer on
    your foreheads sail to that un-
    named shore.

We have known sins and evils every
    day and death we have known;
They pass over our world like clouds
    mocking us with their transient
    lightning laughter.

Suddenly they have stopped, become a
    prodigy,
And men must stand before them
    saying:
"We do not fear you, O Monster! for
    we have lived every day by con-
    quering you,
"And we die with the faith that Peace
    is true, and Good is true, and true
    is the eternal One!"

If the Deathless dwell not in the heart
    of death,
If glad wisdom bloom not bursting the
    sheath of sorrow,
If sin do not die of its own revealment,
If pride break not under its load of
    decorations,
Then whence comes the hope that
    drives these men from their homes
    like stars rushing to their death in
    the morning light?
Shall the value of the martyrs' blood

and mothers' tears be utterly lost
in the dust of the earth, not buying
Heaven with their price?
And when Man bursts his mortal
bounds, is not the Boundless revealed that moment?

LXXXV

THE SONG OF THE
DEFEATED

My Master has bid me while I stand at
the roadside, to sing the song of Defeat,
for that is the bride whom He woos in
secret.

She has put on the dark veil, hiding
her face from the crowd, but the jewel
glows on her breast in the dark.

She is forsaken of the day, and God's
night is waiting for her with its lamps
lighted and flowers wet with dew.

She is silent with her eyes down-
cast; she has left her home behind her,
from her home has come that wailing in
the wind.

But the stars are singing the love-

song of the eternal to a face sweet
with shame and suffering.

The door has been opened in the
lonely chamber, the call has sounded,
and the heart of the darkness throbs
with awe because of the coming tryst.

LXXXVI

THANKSGIVING

THOSE who walk on the path of pride crushing the lowly life under their tread, covering the tender green of the earth with their footprints in blood;

Let them rejoice, and thank thee, Lord, for the day is theirs.

But I am thankful that my lot lies with the humble who suffer and bear the burden of power, and hide their faces and stifle their sobs in the dark.

For every throb of their pain has pulsed in the secret depth of thy night, and every insult has been gathered into thy great silence.

And the morrow is theirs.

O Sun, rise upon the bleeding hearts blossoming in flowers of the morning, and the torchlight revelry of pride shrunken to ashes.

Printed in the United States of America